The Idea Lifestyle Bundle

An Effective System to Fulfill Dreams, Create Successful Business Ideas, and Become a World-Class Impromptu Speaker in Record Time

Andrii Sedniev

The Idea Lifestyle Bundle

An Effective System to Fulfill Dreams, Create Successful Business Ideas, and Become a World-Class Impromptu Speaker in Record Time

Published by Andrii Sedniev

Copyright © 2014 by Andrii Sedniev

ISBN 978-1-49960-143-5

First printing, 2014

All rights reserved. No part of this book may be reproduced in any form or by any electronic or mechanical means including information storage and retrieval systems – except in the case of brief quotations in articles or reviews – without the permission in writing from its publisher, Andrii Sedniev.

www.AndriiSedniev.com

PRINTED IN THE UNITED STATES OF AMERICA

Contents

The Achievement Factory

INTRODUCTION 1

HAPPINESS 2
    Happiness theory 2
    3 keys to an exciting life 5

YOUR LIFE IS IN YOUR HANDS 8
    Self-responsibility for your life 8
    Believe that you can and will achieve a goal 10
    Commitment to achieve a goal 12

CREATE A DREAM LIST 15
    Allow yourself to dream and have a desire 15
    100 dreams exercise 16

PRIORITIZATION 23
    Prioritize goals and be ready to pay the price 23
    3 super-productivity questions 26

HOW TO SET GOALS 28
    Specific and measurable goal 28
    Set achievable goals 31

3 TIMEFRAMES FOR GOALS 33
    Create a compelling vision 33
    Process goals 34
    Set a task for a day 36

VISUALIZATION 39
    What is visualization? 39
    Benefits of visualization 40

VISUALIZATION MAGIC FORMULA 43

POSITIVE THINKING 46
LAW OF ATTRACTION 46
PUT YOUR BRAIN ON A POSITIVE DIET 47
ELIMINATE NEGATIVE THOUGHTS 52

STRATEGY 58
A PLAN FOR ACHIEVING A GOAL 58
MEASURE PROGRESS 60
A PERFECT STRATEGY IS A FLEXIBLE STRATEGY 62
ONE STEP CLOSER TO THE GOAL 63

TAKE MASSIVE ACTION TOWARDS THE GOAL 66
LAW OF INERTIA 66
TAKE MASSIVE DIRECTED ACTION NOW 68
FOCUS ATTENTION 70
SET A DEADLINE 73

FAILURES AND PERSISTENCE 75
FAILURES ARE YOUR FRIENDS 75
LIFE'S PERSISTENCE TEST 77

FUEL FOR ACHIEVING GOALS 80
BURNING DESIRE TO ACHIEVE A GOAL 80
BIG WHAT 83
BIG WANT 86
BIG WHY 87
EMOTIONAL VISUALIZATION TEST 90
ENJOY WHAT YOU DO AS AN EXCITING GAME 92
MAKE ACHIEVING GOALS A GAME 93
SUCCESS BREEDS SUCCESS 94
SUCCESS LOG AND VIRTUAL SUPPORT GROUP 96
SUPPORT OF OTHER PEOPLE IN REACHING YOUR GOAL 98

LAST 5 MINUTES OF THE DAY 101

- Celebrate success and reward yourself 101
- Daily progress and daily plan 102

THE IDEA LIFESTYLE 105
- Think and Rest 105
- Expose yourself to new experiences 108
- Train creative muscles 110

FINAL CHECKLIST 113

The Business Idea Factory

INTRODUCTION 119

CREATIVE BRAIN VS. ANALYTICAL BRAIN 121
- Activate your super-fast brain 121
- Walt Disney strategy 122
- I just need one big idea 123

PROGRAMMING THE MIND 127
- During the day 127
- Before you sleep 129
- Glass of water technique 130

SET A TASK 132
- Ask the right question 132
- Pyramid of problems 135

THINK AND REST 139
- Think and Rest technique 139
- Incubation period 142
- Think about different problems simultaneously 143
- Think in pictures 145

QUANTITY OVER QUALITY OF IDEAS 147
- Avoid making decisions based on past experience 147
- Quantity equals quality 149

  Set ideas quota 151
  Set constraints and think inside the box 152

ESSENCE OF IDEAS 155
  Lesson from the Market 155
  Combine ideas 157
  Copy ideas 161
  Adopt ideas 164
  Early adopters win 165
  Think differently 167

RAW MATERIALS FOR IDEAS 168
  Why you need raw materials 168
  Expose yourself to new experiences 169

WRITE IDEAS DOWN 171

BELIEFS OF THE WORLD-CLASS INNOVATOR 175
  Belief and desire 175
  Visualization 176

RELOCATE TO A HIGH-PERFORMANCE STATE 179

GENERATING IDEAS IS A GAME 183

IDEA REFINEMENT 186
  Idea evolution 186
  Don't strive to be perfect, strive for continuous improvement 187

MODIFYING AN EXISTING PRODUCT OR SERVICE 188
  Transformer 188
  SCAMPER 189

MISTAKES LEAD TO PROGRESS 193
  Creativity is a probability game 193
  Failures are a valuable experience 194

BECOME AN ACCIDENTAL ENTREPRENEUR	195

PHYSICAL FITNESS, SLEEP AND ENERGY 197

IDEAS-STIMULATING ENVIRONMENT 199

WHERE TO THINK BEST	199
MINDLESS ACTIVITIES	203
IDEAS BREED IDEAS	205

WHEN PEOPLE MEET, MAGIC HAPPENS 208

CONVERSATION IS A CRADLE OF IDEAS	208
ENGAGE OTHER PEOPLE TO GIVE YOU IDEAS	209

FILTERING AND EXECUTING IDEAS 211

3 CATEGORIES TECHNIQUE	211
CREATIVE BUDDY	212
IMPLEMENT IDEAS WITH LITTLE RISK	213
"100, 20, 5, 1" RULE	214

ENDURE OPPOSITION AND FRUSTRATIONS 216

GREAT IDEAS FACE OPPOSITION	216
BE PERSISTENT. CREATIVE THINKING IS A MARATHON	218

CREATIVITY HABIT 221

TRAIN CREATIVE MUSCLES	221
DEVELOP A CREATIVITY HABIT	223

FINAL CHECKLIST 225

Magic of Impromptu Speaking

WHY LEARN IMPROMPTU SPEAKING? 231

WHAT IS MAGIC OF IMPROMPTU SPEAKING? 233

BEST IMPROVISATION ISN'T IMPROVISATION ... 235

THE BIGGEST SECRET OF IMPROMPTU SPEAKING ... 239

RELOCATE TO A HIGH-PERFORMANCE STATE 242

HOW TO THINK ON YOUR FEET 246

  Stop internal dialogue 246
  Beliefs of the world-class impromptu speaker 247
  Yes and 250
  The rule of the first thought 251
  How do I find time for thinking? 252
  Exercises for thinking on your feet 254

DECIDE WHICH QUESTION TO ANSWER 258

TRANSITIONS 262

  Exercises for transitions 262

STRUCTURE OF THE IMPROMPTU SPEECH 266

  Opening 266
  Body of the speech 268
  Conclusion 269

3 MAGIC IMPROMPTU SPEAKING FRAMEWORKS 270

  Tell a story 270
  PEEP 273
  Position, Action, Benefit 274

STORYTELLING 276

  Details tell a story 276
  Dialogue 277
  Conflict 278
  Exercises for storytelling 279

TAKE A STAND 283

DELIVERY TECHNIQUES 284

  Be genuine 284
  Be energetic 285

GESTURES 286

FEAR OF IMPROMPTU SPEAKING 288

HUMOR 291
THE STRUCTURE OF THE JOKE 291
EXAGGERATION AND DIALOGUE 292

AN IMPROMPTU SPEECH NEEDS TO BE SUCCINCT 294

BE SIMPLE 296

DON'T STRIVE TO BE PERFECT 298

4 LEVELS OF WORLD-CLASS IMPROMPTU SPEAKING 299

ADDITIONAL TIPS 303

WHERE TO FIND MATERIAL FOR IMPROMPTU SPEECHES? 306

STAGES OF LEARNING 309

WHERE TO PRACTICE? 312

FINAL CHECKLIST 314

LET'S PUT EVERYTHING TOGETHER 315

DON'T STOP UNTIL… 319

FINAL THOUGHTS 323

TOP 100 TABLE TOPIC QUESTIONS FOR PRACTICE 324

WHAT TO READ NEXT? 330

BIOGRAPHY 333

The Achievement Factory

How to Fulfill Your Dreams and Make Life an Adventure

Andrii Sedniev

Dedications

This book and my love are dedicated to Olena, my wife and partner, who makes every day in life worthwhile. Thank you for supporting me on every stage of development of *The Achievement Factory* and giving encouragement when I needed it the most. Without you, this book might never have been finished.

I also want to dedicate this book to all past students of *The Achievement Factory* who by their success inspire me to become a better person every day.

Introduction

Imagine that you have a magic Aladdin lamp and every time you rub it a genie appears and says, "I will fulfill any of your desires." Whether you say, "I want to become a millionaire," "I want to travel around the world," "I want to get married," or "I want to lose weight," the genie will fulfill your wish. How would your life change if you had such a lamp?

Of course magic lamps exist only in fairytales but you can become your own genie and fulfill your dreams whenever you want if you have a big enough desire and use an effective strategy. The Achievement Factory is an effective and easy-to-use system for fulfilling dreams no matter how big. It is based on many years of research of principles that high achievers use to generate excellent ideas, take massive action without procrastination and finish every day successfully. Thousands of Achievement Factory students have noticed that after implementation of this system, they achieve their dreams with almost 100% probability and their path towards achievements became several times shorter.

After you begin using the principles of the Achievement Factory, every day will bring you closer to fulfillment of your dreams, and this progress will breathe happiness and adventures into your life. I hope that what you learn in this book will change your life for the better as it changed the lives of thousands of people who use the Achievement Factory system daily to fulfill their dreams. Let's begin our journey.

Happiness

Happiness theory

I have met many people who were satisfied with their lives, but nobody as happy as Jason. In his 48 years, he has built a company that made him a multimillionaire, lived happily for 25 years with his wife, traveled around the world for 365 days, climbed Mt. Everest, won a national dancing competition and if I continue this list we will have enough material for several adventure novels. But what impressed me the most about Jason was the happiness that he radiates. When he speaks he is always smiling, he is passionate about life and genuinely interested in the person he talks to, and this energy of happiness is contagious. Once I asked, "Jason, what is the secret of your happiness?" and Jason replied:

"When you ask 'What is happiness?' the majority of people give a quite vague definition and as a result don't have a clear understanding of what, specifically, they can do today in order to increase the amount of happiness in their life. The secret of my happiness lies in a clear understanding of what happiness is. 'Happiness is the emotion of progress towards a desirable goal.' Numerous psychologists agree that working on your own goals and achieving small successes daily is what makes your life happy.

"Somebody wants to become a millionaire, somebody wants to travel around the world, somebody wants to get married, somebody wants to raise children, somebody wants to get a promotion at work, somebody wants to learn a foreign language and somebody wants to make a cozy interior in the house. For happiness the nature of your goal doesn't matter, what matters is that you really want to achieve it and that you regularly make progress.

"Sometimes you can hear from people who don't understand what happiness is: 'Be happy with what you already have.' This basically means: 'Don't ever be happy.' A human always wants more, this is our nature, and making progress towards desirable goals is a prerequisite for happiness. My rule of thumb, Jason's rule says: 'If you want to be happy, set a goal, give yourself what you want as quickly as possible and then set a new goal. Never suppress your dreams and desires.'

"Those people who never experience small victories fall into the opposite state of happiness called depression. Psychologists from the University of Liverpool have found that people with depression either don't have goals or their goals are so general that it is impossible to make regular progress towards achieving them. Of course there are unnatural sources of happiness such as drugs, alcohol, chocolate, extreme sports or smoking, however they give a very short-term feeling of happiness and for a cost of severely affecting health and long term happiness.

"When young children play computer games they regularly make progress by getting from one level to another, by winning battles or gaining points. These accomplishments allow children to regularly experience a sense of satisfaction, accomplishment and victory. This concentrated emotion of progress leads to a release of endorphins in the brain and feeling of happiness. Computer games are a simulation of the happy life in the real world, and that's why they are so popular among kids. If you use the concept of regular achievements from computer games, you will become both a screenwriter and a hero of your life and will experience happy moments more often. I perceive my life as a 'computer game' and the reason for my happiness is the progress I make daily on the way to the goals I really want to achieve.

"Many people think they will become happy only after certain event in their life. They say: 'I will become happy once I win a million dollars in a lottery,' 'I will become happy once I win an Olympic gold medal,' 'I will become happy once I graduate from Harvard University' or 'I will be happy once I get married.' Unfortunately for them when this particular event happens the happiness doesn't last long, they quickly get used to what they already have and begin to want more. And it's normal, because everyone wants to be happy and the recipe for happiness is always getting more of what you want and don't have.

"Remember that you are happy not because of what you already have achieved but from the progress you make towards a desirable goal. Not your marital status, bank account or the size of a house give the feeling of happiness but PROGRESS. For example, a person who earns $1,000 per month is equally happy while making progress towards the goal of earning $2,000 per month as a person who earns $1M while making progress towards the goal of earning $2M. The fact that progress equals happiness can be explained by our brain's reward system which releases dopamine after we make measurable progress towards a goal in order to encourage our effort towards accumulating desirable achievements in our life.

"It's also critical to remember that happiness isn't just about making progress, but it's about making progress towards the desirable goal. If you are pursuing a goal that doesn't inspire you and isn't the one you truly want to achieve, then you will experience no joy from progress and accomplishment.

"Andrii, the greatest need of the human is a sense of purpose in life and making regular progress towards desirable goals gives you a sense of purpose. The reason I am happy is because I experience progress and celebrate success daily. Just like children are addicted to computer games I am addicted to life, because I am happy and it feels great."

Happiness comes to those who are moving toward something they want very much to happen. – Earl Nightingale

Look for a situation in which your work will give you as much happiness as your spare time. – Pablo Picasso

If you want to be happy, set a goal that commands your thoughts, liberates your energy, and inspires your hopes. – Andrew Carnegie, the richest man in America in the early 1900s

3 keys to an exciting life

Have you ever observed the excitement of young children when they open their Christmas presents? The experience of playing with wrapping paper and opening a present often brings them much more joy than a present itself. Both for children and adults, experiences impact their happiness much more than physical possessions. Although buying a new toy, a watch or a car brings short-term satisfaction, experiences bring satisfaction that lasts far longer. Many people who have a lot of money are unhappy, however those people who have a lot of positive experiences are always happy. Gather your own fortune of experiences, because experiences are more valuable than gold and make life happy. Over the course of my life I have met hundreds of people who live lives full of adventures and asked them, "What recommendation can you give to a person who wants to make his or her life more exciting?" Although these people were very different they told me very similar things, and their recommendations can be summarized in just 3 points.

Firstly, live your life as an adventure story. You are both a writer and a main character of the book describing the story of your life, and if the plot is interesting you will be excited to wake up every morning and take part in adventures. Deliberately fill your life with chapter after chapter of amazing life experiences and magical moments that fascinate you. Live your life so that when you grow old and tell a story of your life to your great-grandchildren, they will listen in awe and then say to their friends at school, "My great-grandfather (or great-grandmother) is cool!" Live your life as an adventure story and you will have an exciting life.

Secondly, live your life as a competition. Raise your standards and aim for continual progress in important areas of your life. No matter in which area of life you want to become better, today you compete with yesterday's you and tomorrow you will compete with today's you. If you win in this competition regularly you will notice progress, you will admire yourself and experience plenty of happy moments. Everybody who is doing well today in any area of life was once doing poorly and got to where he or she is today by making small wins regularly. If you live your life as a competition and become a little bit better every day you will fulfill all your dreams and have an exciting life.

Finally, live your life as an exploration. Explore the world by doing what you have never done before, by visiting places you have never been to before, by meeting people you haven't known before. The biggest breakthroughs in life happen when you expand your comfort zone and explore the world beyond the border of what you are familiar with. Often people are afraid of going outside of their comfort zone, however in 99% of cases what they fear isn't dangerous at all. Ask yourself: "What do I fear to do, but will bring me joy if I do it?" Live your life as an exploration, expand your comfort zone, experiment and you will have an exciting life.

Everyone, once in a while, asks himself or herself: "How can I make my life more exciting?" This question is extremely important because answers that you come to may impact one of the most important things in life – your happiness. Nobody can answer this question besides you but I hope that these 3 recommendations from people who already found their answers for themselves will help you to come up with valuable ideas.

Life isn't about finding yourself. Life is about creating yourself. – George Bernard Shaw

The person who has lived the most is not the one with the most years but the one with the richest experiences. – Jean-Jacques Rousseau

Twenty years from now you will be more disappointed by the things that you didn't do than by the ones you did do so throw off the bowlines. Sail away from the safe harbor. Catch the trade winds in your sails. Explore. Dream. Discover. – Mark Twain

Your life is in your hands

Self-responsibility for your life

Imagine that you are listening to a speaker in a room where the temperature is extremely low. All the people in the audience are freezing, however don't do anything about it. They just complain. Somebody says: "Oh, I am freezing!" And somebody answers, "Everybody is freezing. Not only you." Somebody says, "I didn't choose this room for the conference. It's the organizer's fault." And somebody answers, "Today is just an unlucky day for all of us." Finally a speaker says, "It's all winter's fault! If there was no winter it wouldn't be cold in the room."

You may think: "It doesn't make sense to suffer the cold for no reason. Most people would wear a jacket, drink hot coffee, do physical exercises, leave the room or ask a speaker to turn on the heating. Of course people would do at least something to eliminate the discomfort."

You are absolutely right. Of course most people understand that they can't control external circumstances such as the weather. The only thing they can do is react to them by taking certain action. If you are cold you would rather wear a jacket, a hat and gloves than just complain about the weather.

When you don't have what you want or what you dream about, you feel discomfort. Isn't this situation similar to the cold audience? You might say, "I don't have what I want because my manager doesn't value me, because the economy is bad, because competition is tough, because I am too old, because I am too young, because my partner deceived me, because my parents weren't rich or because I was born in the wrong country." You know what is the saddest? The saddest is that you will find many people saying, "Yes, life is tough. Yes, all these circumstances are the reasons you don't have what you want. Put up with the fact that you will never live the life of your dreams."

The truth is that no one can control external circumstances. No one can control age, the economy, the competition, the weather or the behavior of other people. The only thing you can control is your actions. No matter how bad the circumstances are it is always possible to get what you want; however, to get it you need to believe in the statement: "I am 100% responsible for everything that happens in my life. My actions, not the circumstances, create my future."

There are people who without legs win running competitions. There are people who without higher education become scientists. There are people who without starting capital create successful businesses. However, there are no people who get what they want by making excuses and blaming the circumstances.

People who are successful always talk about what they want and what they will do to achieve it. People who aren't talk about circumstances that don't let them live the life they want. Your life is in your hands only and the only person who can make it either miserable or exceptional is YOU. Whether you succeed or fail say to yourself: "I am 100% responsible for everything that happens in my life. My actions, not the circumstances, create my future." If you truly believe in this statement you are already on the highway towards the life of your dreams.

Ninety-nine percent of all failures come from people who have a habit of making excuses. – George Washington Carver, botanist who discovered over 325 uses for the peanut

You must take personal responsibility. You cannot change the circumstances, the seasons, or the wind, but you can change yourself. – Jim Rohn, America's foremost business philosopher

Believe that you can and will achieve a goal

For thousands of years after the first Olympic Games in ancient Greece it was firmly believed that running a mile in under 4 minutes was not only impossible, but also dangerous. Doctors and scientists claimed, "Even if a human ever runs a sub-four minute mile his or her heart would explode." Imagine, how hard you would push yourself in training and competitions as a runner, if you shared the belief that your heart could explode?

Then in the 1950s, in England, a medical student named Roger Bannister, as part of his medical research, studied anatomy and physiology of the human body and looked for medical evidence of a physical limitation to run a sub-four minute mile. Roger came to the conclusion that not only will the heart not explode, but also that a human is more than capable of running the mile in less than 4 minutes. He was so confident in his findings that he announced to the world, "I personally will break the record and prove that running a 4-minute mile is possible!"

On May 6, 1954, in Oxford, Roger Bannister made his mark in history. He broke the world record and ran a mile in 3 minutes and 59.4 seconds. Unbelievably, just 46 days later a runner from Australia ran a mile in 3 minutes and 58.0 seconds, and within the next 5 years 20 more runners ran a mile in less than 4 minutes. What had been considered impossible for thousands of years was accomplished by 20 people within 5 years after they changed their belief.

Some people think, "I doubt that I can achieve my goal." As a result, this doubt prevents their subconscious minds from generating ideas, keeps them from pushing themselves hard enough and eventually they give up after meeting a first obstacle and say: "I was right when I said that I couldn't achieve my goal." If you believe that you are limited in intelligence, creativity or talent, you will act as if you are indeed limited in that particular area. The biggest reason why people fail is not their lack of abilities but their lack of belief in their abilities. No matter what you believe in, your brain will look for confirmations that you are right and will eventually find them. As Henry Ford said, "Whether you think you can, or you think you can't – you're right."

History has numerous examples of when people, even in the most unfavorable circumstances, achieved their goals: poor people became rich, people with bad health became athletes and people who were considered mentally retarded became scientists. If you say, "I have 100% confidence that I will achieve my goal," you will find a solution, you will take massive action, you will overcome any obstacles and after achieving a goal will say, "I was right when I said that I can achieve my goal!"

The magical invocation that successful people use to achieve their goals is "I can." On the way to your goal tell yourself "I can" every day, and if anybody ever says "You can't" say "I can." You can achieve literally whatever you want if you have a big enough desire and belief that you can.

If you want to be successful, it's just this simple. Know what you are doing. Love what you are doing. And believe in what you are doing. – Will Rogers

The only thing that stands between a man and what he wants from life is often merely the will to try it and the faith to believe that it is possible. – Richard M. DeVos

The future belongs to those who believe in the beauty of their dreams. – Eleanor Roosevelt

Commitment to achieve a goal

In 331 BC, with an army of 35,000 men, Alexander the Great arrived at the shores of Persia to fight with Persian king Darius III. Upon arriving, soldiers from Alexander's army realized that they were greatly outnumbered by the 200,000-member army of the enemy. They pleaded to their young leader: "Alexander, we should delay the attack. Let's go back home to return later with more men." As the legend says, Alexander ordered his soldiers to burn their boats and said: "We go home in Persian ships, or we die!" Alexander's soldiers realized that the only way to survive was to win. They committed to return home alive and in one of the most dramatic battles of all times defeated the Persians.

There is a significant difference between, "I wish to achieve my goal" and "I am committed to achieve my goal." If you wish to achieve your goal it means, "I will accept it if it falls into my lap." You will do what is easy and convenient on the way to the goal, but once faced with difficulties you will find excuses and give up. However, if you decide to be committed, it means, "I will achieve my goal no matter what. Failure is not an option." Commitment is when you have burned the ships and there is no room for a backup in your mind.

Since I graduated high school, my dream was to pass the Cisco Certified Internetwork Expert certification (CCIE), which even today is considered the most prestigious and difficult IT certification to obtain in the world. This certification is considered so difficult not only because of the enormous amount of information you need to know but also because of the extremely difficult lab part of the exam where you need to configure a network of 10 devices according to the suggested scenario within 8 hours. After 3 years of intensive preparation and one day before I was supposed to fly to Brussels to take my chance in the lab part of the exam, my mother asked: "What if you don't pass the exam in the first attempt? What is your plan B?"

I said, "Mom, I will definitely pass! Since I don't have a full-time job like the majority of engineers who attempt to pass CCIE, I won't have enough money to finance the second attempt. I will also not have enough time to prepare for the second attempt. I have been practicing for 16 hours a day for 4 months in the last phase of my preparation. I didn't attend classes at the university the entire months of September and October and have received a notification that I might be expelled. I don't have any other option rather than to pass now. I don't have a plan B." After I passed the exam I looked back at everything I did including the possible and the impossible on the way to my dream and realized: "My burning desire to earn a CCIE and a 100% commitment were the reasons for my success. If, again, I have such a burning desire and commitment to achieve another dream, nothing will be able to stop me."

Having a plan B is dangerous, because if you have it you won't do 100% of what you can to implement your plan A. You may stop trying to achieve a goal after the first few failures and eventually end up with this plan B. When you are committed, you give your mind an order to think about solutions and give yourself no space to think about excuses. The secret of incredible commitment is simple: "Determine which dream could have the biggest positive impact on your happiness. Make a promise to yourself to fulfill this dream no matter how difficult it is."

Create a dream list

Allow yourself to dream and have a desire

Imagine that you are 90 years old. You sit comfortably in an armchair and around you sit all your children, grandchildren and great-grandchildren. They say, "Granny, Granny! (Or Grandpa, Grandpa!) You lived such a fascinating life. Your life is one of the greatest adventures that we have ever heard about. Everything you ever dreamed about came true. Please, tell us one more time how it all began."

You smile and begin your story, "Well, many years ago I found an ancient Aladdin lamp. When I rubbed it a genie appeared and said, 'This is a magic lamp and I am an almighty genie. I will fulfill everything you ask me for. And I can fulfill not 3, not 5 but an unlimited number of your desires. The only thing I can't do is to decide what you truly want.'

"I said, 'That's amazing, genie. I will certainly ask you for many things to turn my life into the life of my dreams. I didn't ever expect to meet you and don't have a list of my desires ready for you. Can I take an hour to clarify what I want and write down all my desires?'

"And the genie said, 'Sure. And to help you clarify all your desires I will share with you a "100 dreams exercise." This exercise is extremely effective and will help you to identify everything you want at this point. Once you complete this exercise and clearly know your desires, we will be already halfway towards making your life an adventure. The dream that you don't know you have will never get fulfilled, that's why the time you spend thinking about your desires is perhaps the most effectively spent time in your life."

100 dreams exercise

Write down all your dreams

Your task is to write down a minimum of 100 desires that you would ask a genie to fulfill if you had a magic lamp. This could be literally anything: small desires, big desires, physical possessions, relationships, achievements or experiences. Imagine what your perfect life would look like and think about which desires would bring you from where you are to the life in your imagination. Spend at least 1 hour thinking about what you would want if there were no limitations and you could get and achieve anything. Don't worry about making this list perfect, as you will be able to change or update it in the future. The most important thing in this exercise is the quantity of desires, which should be not less than 100.

You will probably write the first 20 desires really quickly because they are at the top of your mind. Once you exhaust desires you have thought about before, your subconscious will begin really thinking. Desires that are between numbers 60 and 100 are usually the most original desires that you haven't considered before.

According to research done by Dominican University, people who just think about their goals achieve them with 43% probability. People who not only think about their goals but also write down their goals achieve them with 61%

probability. Finally, people who write down their goals, create action plans and check progress weekly increase their chances for success to 76%. Isn't that impressive that just by thinking about what you want you can achieve your goal with 43% probability and writing down your goal increases this probability by another 20%? Later in the book you will learn principles that will allow you to raise this probability to 100%, however at this point you need to understand that clearly knowing what you want and putting it on paper is perhaps the most important step towards the life of your dreams.

This exercise is extremely important to make your life more exciting as it allows you to realize what you want, and realizing what you want is already at least 50% of success. Thousands of successful people around the world achieved their dreams using principles from this book and I promise that you will achieve anything you truly want if you use the same principles. You will become your own genie.

3 magic questions for identifying desires

Did you write all 100 desires in the previous exercise? The more desires you write down, the more you clarify for yourself what could make your life more exciting. The following 3 questions are my favorites because they are extremely effective for generating ideas for your life desires list.

1) How would you live your life if you had a billion dollars?

People often limit their desires by thinking about their current salary, savings or job. Thinking about this question will allow you to identify what you would do, have or be if money wasn't a problem. To live the life of your dreams, you first need to understand how the life of your dreams looks.

Once you identify clearly what you really dream about, you will be able to develop a plan for fulfilling a dream no matter what your current circumstances are.

2) If you were guaranteed success, what would you do?

People often limit their desires by thinking about potential failures and obstacles. This question will allow you to decide which desires would make your life more fulfilling if you were guaranteed success. The answers to this question are certainly great candidates for your 100 dreams list and once fulfilled will make your life an exciting adventure.

3) Remember all the moments in your life when you felt alive, excited and happy. How could you bring more such moments to your life?

You have experienced a lot of happy moments in the past that psychologist Abraham Maslow has identified as "peak experiences." One of your aims in life is to enjoy as many happy moments as possible. If you clearly understand what caused these happy moments in the past, you will have ideas for desires that need to be added to your dreams list in order to experience more of these peak experiences in the future.

I have tested numerous questions in identifying the true desires of my students, and these 3 questions proved to be the most effective for many years. Ask yourself these questions to come up with great ideas for your dreams.

Four areas of goals setting

There are 4 major areas of life that you need to develop in order to live a happy and fulfilling life: body and health, career and business, socialization and family, and personal development.

1) Body and health

The healthy body is the vehicle that can get you to a happy and fulfilling life. The desires from this area are related to improvement of your health or body. For example: "I want to become more energetic after losing 20 pounds," "I want to become more flexible by attending yoga for 3 months," "I want to gain more control over my body by learning how to dance salsa," "I want to become more energetic by developing a habit of stretching every morning," "I want to be able to do 25 pull-ups" or "I want to make my daily diet more healthy by excluding certain foods."

2) Career and business

The career and business section covers your financial goals, the way you want to earn money, to self-realize and to contribute to society. Are you doing what you love each day to earn money? Do you have enough money to live the life of your dreams? What do you want to achieve that will make you proud and self-fulfilled? Desires from this section will help you to earn more money, to have fun doing it and to feel that what you do has a purpose and meaning.

3) Socialization and family

Social desires are targeted at improving your relationships with family or your interactions with friends or strangers. For example, "Take family on vacation to Hawaii," "Take parents to the restaurant," "Meet 20 new people in the city I am moving to," "Attend a conference and start a conversation with at least 10 strangers," or "Sign up for dance classes together with a friend." Social goals are just anything that will allow you to either meet new people or to maintain relationships with people who you already know.

4) Personal development

Personal development desires are any desires that will enrich you intellectually or spiritually. For example: "I want to travel through Europe for one month," "I want to write a novel," "I want to read at least 20 nonfiction books within a year," "I want to learn a new skill" or " I want to overcome a fear of public speaking." Being in a constant state of personal development keeps you growing.

Depending on your preferences and time in your life, you may dedicate more time to reaching desires in one area than in the other 3, however you can't completely ignore any of these 4 areas. If you devote all your efforts to developing your career, you may feel unhappy if you have family problems or don't have a family. If you have an amazing family, you may feel unhappy because you have poor health and little energy. If you have great income, an excellent family and excellent health, you may not feel completely happy if you are not pursuing any desires in the personal development area.

You can have more desires in areas that you are most interested in, however remember that you need to have at least some desires in each of the areas in order to have a happy and fulfilling life. These 4 areas also greatly support each other. For example, if you have great social connections and a happy family life, you will be more successful in your work. If you have excellent health, you will have a better mood and will have better family relationships. If you invest time in personal development, you might be more successful in your work and at building social connections.

Now return to the 100 dreams exercise and write down more desires in areas that you haven't covered thoroughly yet. Being in the constant flow of setting and achieving goals in each of the 4 life areas is a key to a happy, adventurous and successful life.

Creating dreams is a continuous process

After you have completed the 100 dreams exercise and written down on paper all the dreams you could come up with, you need to think periodically about what else you may want and add new dreams to this list. Remember that an exceptional life consists of two parts: coming up with new desires, and making them a reality. If you want to make your life an adventure, you need to understand that dreaming and coming up with new desires is a continuous process.

Make it a habit to spend at least 15 minutes every 2 weeks thinking about "What else would I want if everything were possible or what else could I ask for if I had a magic wand?" You will realize that during each of these sessions new ideas will come to your mind.

Firstly, when you think about what you want regularly, you activate your subconscious mind and it thinks about your desires 24/7. If you think about what you want twice a month for 15 minutes it doesn't mean that your subconscious thinks about your desires for 30 minutes in total, it means it thinks about them 30 days round the clock. Thinking regularly about desires for short periods of time will give you far more ideas than a single super-long creative session.

Secondly, your life experiences are raw materials and inspiration for new ideas, which are essentially combinations of old ideas. As you live your life, fulfill desires and experience different events your subconscious gains more data for creativity and will be able to create excellent fresh ideas for desires that it wasn't able to create before.

Happiness is a process of setting goals and achieving them, however to achieve goals you first need to clearly understand what you want. Even the most experienced shooter can't hit the target if he or she doesn't see it. Every time you absolutely clearly understand what your desire is, you are already halfway towards making it happen.

Every once in a while think about your desires and add ideas to your dream list. Remember that in order to live the life of your dreams you first need to clearly understand how exactly the life of your dreams looks. Ask yourself, "What do I want?" and listen to what your inner voice says. This conversation needs to take place regularly to keep your dreams list up to date with goals that are most desirable at the current stage of your life. Creating and fulfilling desires is a continuous process.

Don't limit yourself. Many people limit themselves to what they think they can do. You can go as far as your mind lets you. – Mary Kay Ash

Realize what you really want. It stops you from chasing butterflies and puts you to work digging gold. – William Moulton Marsden

The indispensable first step to getting the things you want out of life is this: decide what you want. – Ben Stein, actor and author

Prioritization

Prioritize goals and be ready to pay the price

When I was 7, at the school where I studied, there was a casting call for the boys' choir. I enjoyed singing so after classes I went to the school cafeteria and asked a lady who was sitting at the piano, "How can I participate in the casting?" She hit a key on the piano and asked me to sing the note "Do." I tried my best to repeat the sound, but could see that the lady didn't like how I sang. She hit another key on the piano and asked me to repeat the note "Re." I tried my best but could see that she again didn't like what I did. After several more attempts she said, "You have no ear for music. Unfortunately, I can't recommend you to the choir." At the age of 21, when I was a highly paid IT engineer, I recalled my childhood desire to sing and thought, "In my childhood I couldn't study in the free school choir because I didn't pass the casting. Today, I can afford a private singing coach and he or she will teach me whether I have an ear for music or not."

After my first class with one of the best private singing coaches in the city, she asked: "Andrii, how much do you want to sing? You see, because of your natural ear for music you will make progress much slower than my other students. You will never be able to become a great singer but probably after 1,000 hours of practice you will be able to sing in a circle of friends. Please think and let me know if you are ready to pay this price for your goal."

At home the following conversation took place in my head: "I am very purposeful and if I decide to achieve a goal of becoming a better singer I will achieve it no matter what. But is this my first-priority goal? No. I want to become a better dancer, learn German and develop my business more than I want to become a better singer and if I invest 1,000 hours in one of these goals right now I would be happier. Is becoming a better singer worth its price for me? No, 1,000 hours is too expensive for the goal of being able to sing in a circle of friends. What should I do to become happier? I should focus on goals I want to achieve the most and on the goals that I am ready to pay for with the necessary amount of time, money and willpower."

Imagine that you enter a goals supermarket and see a price tag next to each goal you have to pay for with your time and resources: To be able to do 100 pull-ups – 200 hours of training on the bar. Become an Olympic Games gold medal winner – 6 years of training, 4 hours per day at least 310 days a year. Become a world famous violin player – 10,000 hours of practice. Become a multimillionaire – 20 years of intense work without weekends, thousands of failures, rejections and disappointments. Travel around the world – 6 months of time and $30,000.

Your wallet has a limited amount of hours and resources. Even if you are extremely purposeful and wealthy you can't buy everything in the goals supermarket and need to prioritize your "purchases." For example, if you decide to become an Olympic Games gold medal winner, a world-famous writer and travel around the world, you can't achieve all these goals simultaneously because the number of hours in a day is limited; however, you can achieve them sequentially. Ask yourself, "What one goal is most important for me, and the achieving of which would have the biggest positive impact on my life?" According to research you can effectively work without losing focus only on several major goals simultaneously. Pick your one or two major goals and start pursuing them right now; leave all others for the future.

For each of the goals, you need to determine a price in terms of time and resources and decide if you are ready to pay it or not. For example, everyone may want to become a multimillionaire, but not everyone is ready to pay the price for it that consists of time, disappointments and deprivation of daily pleasures. For most people who want to improve their financial situation, a goal of earning a six-figure salary may be more reasonable in terms of the price they have to pay. Everyone wants to become an Olympic Games gold medal winner but not everyone is ready for the price it costs in terms of hours of training. For most people, a goal of being able to do 100 pull-ups or run a marathon may be more reasonable. Everybody would like to be a world-famous writer, but not everyone is ready to spend 10,000 hours on writing. For most people, writing just one book may be much more compelling.

Once you have created a list of your dreams, prioritize them and determine how much each of them may cost you in terms of time and resources. Choose your highest-priority desires and for each of them ask yourself, "Am I truly committed to pay the price to achieve this goal?" If the answer is yes, begin working towards this goal; there is virtually nothing that can stop you. If you are truly passionate about your goal, paying the price by accomplishing the necessary amount of work to achieve it will be much more pleasurable because you will enjoy the process rather than suffer through it.

If people knew how hard I had to work to gain my mastery, it wouldn't seem wonderful at all. – Michelangelo (Renaissance sculptor and painter, who spent 4 years lying on his back painting the ceiling of the Sistine Chapel)

3 super-productivity questions

If you want to fulfill your desire as soon as possible, you need to increase your productivity. The experience of thousands of successful people shows that if you regularly ask yourself the 3 super-productivity questions below, you will be able to significantly optimize the use of your time.

Occasionally ask yourself the first super-productivity question, "Is this particular action I am doing right now getting me closer to my goal or further away?" There are no neutral actions. Everything you do either gets you closer to the goal or postpones achieving the destination. A study by Vouchercloud.com found that office workers on average are productive only 2 hours and 53 minutes per day. The rest of the time is spent on distractions such as checking social networks, reading news websites or discussing out-of-work activities with colleagues. If after asking this question you switch, at least sometimes, from a distracting activity to an activity that gets you closer to the goal, your productivity will increase.

Ask yourself a second super-performance question, "What is the most valuable use of my time right now?" According to

Pareto principles, 20% of activities bring 80% of results. Make sure that after asking this question you work on the task that makes the biggest progress in the direction of the goal.

A third super-productivity question is, "How can I do what I am doing more effectively?" If you come up with ideas of how to optimize the process you use, how to cut unnecessary steps from the work you do or how to delegate simple tasks, you will manage to do more in less time.

Asking super-productivity questions will allow you to make sure that your actions get you closer to the goal, that your actions produce the biggest result and that your processes are optimized. The more effectively you use your time, the quicker you will achieve your goal and the sooner you will live the life of your dreams.

The things that matter most must never be at the mercy of the things that matter least. – Goethe

How to set goals

Ask any successful person, "How did you get to where you are in life?" He or she will most probably say, "By setting and achieving goals." Once you have decided to fulfill your dream, formulate it as a specific, measurable and achievable goal. Goals serve as a GPS navigator that sets a direction and lets you know whether a particular action or idea takes you closer to the destination or further away. Setting a goal effectively has the biggest impact on whether you achieve what you want or not, because in order to get to the destination you first need to know what this destination is. The most powerful goals are those that are measurable, specific and achievable because they set clearly a direction that needs to be followed in order to achieve them. To shorten a path towards the life of your dreams, make sure that you always set goals that are specific, measurable and achievable.

Specific and measurable goal

Imagine that you have a little genie inside you who can fulfill any of your desires. Whatever you ask the genie for, he will fulfill. However, ask cautiously because this genie is naughty and will fulfill the desires exactly as you formulate them. If there is a way to fulfill your desire and leave you unhappy, be sure the genie will fulfill it this way. For example, you say, "Genie, I want a BIG change in my life." Next year you may have a divorce and this will be a BIG change in your life, just as you asked. If you say, "I want a car," you will get a 20-year-old car. If you say, "I want to significantly lose weight," you will have severe diarrhea.

Imagine that you live in New York, wake up in the morning and decide, "I want to go to the Empire State Building." Whether you decide to go there by car, by subway or by walking you will definitely get there. Why? Firstly, because the address of the Empire State Building is very specifically defined and you will be able to choose the direction of movement properly. Secondly, because you will be able to track your progress and see that with time you are getting closer to the destination. And finally, you will clearly understand whether you already reached your destination or not.

Setting a goal is very similar to getting from point A to point B in the city. If you know very clearly what your goal is, you will always reach the destination because you know its address. Desires are often fulfilled just as if a naughty genie was fulfilling them. The more clearly you formulate your goal, the more likely you will get what you want in a way you want and experience joy after getting it.

Instead of formulating a goal like "I want more money," say "I want to save $50,000." Instead of saying "I want to be fit," say "I want to be able to do 100 pushups." Instead of saying "I want to travel around the world," say "I want to spend a week in Rome." Fifty thousand dollars, 100 pushups and a week in Rome are specific enough goals for you to develop a plan on how to achieve them, to see if your effort got you closer to them and if you already reached them.

Many people make a lot of chaotic movements in their life without having clear goals and then wonder why they don't live the lives of their dreams. People who do indeed live the lives of their dreams always spend enough time to clarify their goals before moving anywhere. No matter how fast they are capable of moving, they always get what they want because every single step brings them closer to the destination.

There is a direct relationship between everything you achieve in life and how clearly you specify your goals, because clarity of your goals impacts the preciseness and effectiveness of your actions. That's why the most important step towards living the life of your dreams is to define as specifically as possible what exactly you want. So specifically that a 7-year-old child could explain what your goal is and determine whether you achieved it or not. It's impossible to hit a target that you can't see, that's why before taking any actions you should ask yourself, "Did I define my goal specifically enough?" and if the answer is yes, think about how you can make it even more specific.

In the absence of clearly-defined goals, we become strangely loyal to performing daily trivia until ultimately we become enslaved by it. – Robert A. Heinlein

If you really know what you want out of life, it's amazing how opportunities will come to enable you to carry them out. – John Goddard, great life adventurer

Everyone wants to improve their life. We can have these big ambitions, but if we don't break those down and set specific goals, we're not ever going to get anywhere. – Crystal Paine

Set achievable goals

When you formulate a goal make sure that the goal is within your control. The only thing you can control in life is you and your actions. Set the goals that depend only on you, not luck, circumstances or other people. For example, if you set a goal "Win a dancing competition," this goal doesn't depend fully on you, it also depends on your competitors and the judges. However if you set a goal "Practice dancing for 200 hours under supervision of a world-famous instructor and 500 hours on my own," this goal is completely under your control.

Also make sure that the goal is theoretically achievable or otherwise you will fail with a 100% guarantee. What is a theoretically unachievable goal then? For example, to earn a million dollars is an achievable goal. But to earn a million dollars next month is a theoretically unachievable goal if your income this month was $1,000 and you don't have a breakthrough idea of how to increase it quickly by 1,000 times. To run a mile in 3 minutes 43 seconds is an achievable goal. But to run a mile in 5 seconds is a theoretically unachievable goal due to limitations of the human body. To learn 10,000 foreign words is an achievable goal. But to learn 10,000 foreign words within 1 day is an unachievable goal if you don't have superpowers.

Sometimes, people set goals they have little control over, or that are theoretically unachievable, and then get disappointed after failure. The worst thing that can happen after failure is that you may lose faith in goal setting, say "Goal setting doesn't work" and stop moving towards making your life exceptional. Set goals that stretch you, but make sure that they are completely under your control and are theoretically achievable. If you do, you will have more motivation to take action towards your goals and as a result will achieve them more often.

A good goal is like a strenuous exercise – it makes you stretch. – Mary Kay Ash

Most people overestimate what they can do in one year and underestimate what they can do in ten years. – Bill Gates

Without goals and plans to reach them, you are like a ship that has set sail with no destination. – Fitzhugh Dodson

3 timeframes for goals

Create a compelling vision

In his research, Dr. Edward Banfield, a Harvard psychologist, wanted to discover why some people become financially independent in the course of their lives and others don't. At the beginning of the research he expected that the answer would lie among such factors as intelligence, education, family background or relationships. However, Dr. Banfield discovered that the single factor that determined success was how far a person projects into the future while taking actions today.

The least successful members of society such as alcoholics or drug addicts have the lowest time perspective. They are focused on short-term pleasures and make decisions about their actions taking into account only how their life might look like in several hours. People who don't reach financial independence make decisions today considering only how their life will look like in a week, a month or a quarter. Successful people have a clear understanding of how they want their future to look in several years and make their decisions today based on this long-term vision. Dr. Banfield discovered that the further you think into the future, the better you make decisions today to make sure that this future becomes a reality and the more successful you become as a result.

Take time to dream and decide what your perfect life would look like in 5 years if everything were possible. Your 5-year vision should be so compelling that simply thinking about it will make you feel goose bumps and put a smile on your face. A clear and exciting vision will stimulate you to take actions today necessary to make it a reality in the future. The lives of happy and successful people are very different: some of them become Olympic Games winners, some build big corporations, some travel around the world, some become fluent in several languages and some become great parents; however, one thing that is common among them is that they all have a clear and compelling vision.

Creating or clarifying a vision is a process that can take you a day, a week or a month, however it is absolutely worth your time and can have an enormous positive impact on your life. If you have decided on a direction for your life, all your actions will move you further in that direction. If you haven't, some of your actions will move you forward, some backwards, some left, some right and eventually you might stay in one place. Knowing clearly how your dream life looks is the most important step towards making your dream life a reality.

Process goals

Besides a compelling vision for the next 1 to 10 years, you should also have a goal for the next 1 to 3 months to get closer to the life of your dreams. If a vision gives a general direction for your life, a process goal is a dream or a part of the dream to accomplish for which you are taking specific actions today. You might ask: "Why do you recommend setting goals for 1- 3 months?"

If you set a goal for one year, it's too far off and you may be enticed to procrastinate. A day is a very short period of time compared to a year, and you might think, "If I do nothing today, it won't be a big problem for meeting a deadline." If however you set a goal for a week, this time frame is too short for you to sense a tangible progress at the end and experience significant satisfaction from the result. That's why a perfect time frame for the goal is 1 to 3 months in order for you to feel that the deadline is close, and that every day matters from one side and to be motivated to take action because the result you can achieve is significant from the other.

For example, if you decide to win a national swimming competition in a year, you might think "Missing just one training won't be a big deal because I will have plenty of time to make it up." If however you set a goal for a week, you will barely be motivated imagining how great a swimmer you will be by achieving it. No matter how intensively you train, a week is a very short period of time to sense significant progress at the end. That's why setting a goal for 1 to 3 months will make you most productive in making your dreams a reality because it will stimulate you to take actions without procrastination and motivate by a compelling possible result.

You might reasonably ask, "But, Andrii, what if my dream takes longer than 3 months to fulfill. What should I do?" If your dream takes longer than 3 months to fulfill, split achieving it into blocks of 3 months because this period of time will make you the most productive and motivated. For example, imagine that you currently earn $1,000 per month and your dream, in a year, is to earn $5,000 per month. Split this goal into 4 sub goals: To earn $1,500 per month in 3 months, to earn $2,250 in 6 months, to earn $3,375 in 9 months and finally $5,000 in 12 months. If you split your goal into blocks of 3 months, you will feel more pressure to take action without procrastination, you will have higher motivation as you will regularly experience intermediate success and as a result you will be much more likely to achieve a goal on time.

The dream life consists of fulfilled dreams and each dream consists of one or more goals. The perfect time frame for the goal is 1 to 3 months. Decide what your goals are for the next 1- to 3-month block and begin pursuing them today.

Set a task for a day

In order to achieve a goal, you need to set a task for the day so that you clearly understand what to do each hour and have motivation to act. For example, if you prepare for swimming competitions, your daily task may be to swim a certain distance. If you create a title for your company, your daily task may be to generate a certain amount of ideas. If you prepare for an exam, your daily task may be to read a certain amount of book pages.

Many people make the mistake of setting long-term goals, however don't split them into clear and measurable daily tasks. As a result, they either feel overwhelmed and don't take actions towards the goal or after months of taking chaotic actions realize that their effort didn't bring the desired results. Split a goal into measurable daily tasks and by accomplishing each of them, you will make small but regular progress towards the destination. Each task you set for the day converts into specific actions that are feasible to accomplish and completely under your control.

People often become depressed and unmotivated if they work towards their goals for months and don't experience intermediate success. The key to maintaining motivation is setting tasks for each day, accomplishing them and celebrating the success. Sometimes the success you achieve will be small, sometimes big, but most important is that you experience joy from accomplishment every single day. If you know that, "In the evening I will recognize and celebrate everything I have accomplished during the day. It will feel great!" this thought will keep you motivated to act right now without procrastination.

Your success in life depends on how much you achieve within a year, the success within a year depends on how much you achieve within a month and your success within a month depends how much you achieve within a day. The task for today converts an abstract goal into specific actions that are within your control as well as motivates you to take them and make progress. As a result, you will be able to finish your day successfully, achieve your goals and eventually make your vision a reality.

When you chop a tree, the strength of your whacks is important but not as important as that they are all directed at the same spot. If they are, the strength of each whack will be accumulated and the tree will eventually fall; otherwise you will spend hours hitting chaotically without any result. The same is true for achieving your dreams. Productivity of your work is important but not as important as that all your actions are taken in the same direction. To maximize the accumulated effect from everything you do, always keep in mind your long-term vision, 1-3 months goal and the task for the day.

The secret of getting ahead is getting started. The secret of getting started is breaking your complex, overwhelming tasks into small manageable tasks, and then starting on the first one. — Mark Twain, celebrated American author and humorist

In essence, if we want to direct our lives, we must take control of our consistent actions. It's not what we do once in a while that shapes our lives, but what we do consistently. — Anthony Robbins

Visualization

What is visualization?

Memories are the replaying of past events in your head and visualization is the replaying of future events in your head. Imagine an event that happened to you last year, last month or yesterday in detail as clearly as possible. Now imagine what you really want to happen to you in the future in detail as clearly as possible. It may be a trip to a foreign country, a purchase of a new house or a big deal in business. Notice that the image quality in your head is the same for the future as for the past, although you were physically present in the past and saw everything with your own eyes, but you have never been in the future. Why does this happen?

When you visualize the future your optic nerve is directly involved and acts as if you were physically seeing what you are imagining. Your brain doesn't see the difference between reality and imagination and believes that what you visualize is indeed happening. When you regularly visualize the goal as already achieved, it creates a conflict in your subconscious mind between what you currently have and what you imagine. As a result, the subconscious does everything possible to resolve this conflict and to turn imaginary pictures into reality. Successful people know the power of visualization and regularly use it as a magic wand to turn their dreams into reality. You might ask, "Why is visualization that powerful?" About that in the next section…

Benefits of visualization

Visualization increases your desire to achieve a goal

Every time you visualize a moment when your goal is achieved you sense how pleasurable this moment will be and as a result increase your desire to achieve the goal. The higher your desire to achieve a goal, the more excited you are to wake up every morning and to take necessary actions in the direction of the goal. Visualizing the dream builds up your desire to make it a reality and this desire motivates you to take massive action without procrastination. If you regularly visualize a goal, your productivity increases and as a result you achieve a goal quicker than without visualization.

Visualization increases focus and directs actions

The rule of focus says: "What you focus your attention on is where your energy flows and what eventually gets done." Your thoughts control your body; the more you think about the goal, the more actions you make relevant to the goal and the faster you move towards achievement of the goal. As American Philosopher William James said, "Your physical actions are simply the outward manifestation of your inner thoughts. What you see in yourself is what you get out of yourself."

Every time you visualize your dream you focus your attention on this dream and simply by doing so increase the amount of actions you take and ideas you generate relevant to this dream. The more often you visualize your dream, the more you focus on this dream and the sooner it will be achieved. Visualization increases your focus and directs your thoughts and actions.

Visualization helps to activate the subconscious to generate ideas

When you work towards a goal, you constantly need ideas: "What actions should I take tomorrow?" "How do I fulfill this task?" "Where can I find the necessary resources?" The subconscious mind is responsible for generating ideas and if you give it a task, it will process thoughts during the day and during the night and eventually will give you solutions for any problem. When you visualize your goal, you give your subconscious a task: "Please create solutions that will help me to achieve my goal." If you don't think about your goal, the subconscious mind stays idle and does nothing. But if you occasionally visualize your goal, you activate your super-powerful subconscious mind to generate continuous flow of ideas and as a result the path towards the goal becomes clearer. The process of goal achievement consists of ideas and actions, and visualization positively influences both these components.

Visualization programs the brain's filter

Every second your brain receives about 10 million bits of information but allows into your awareness only those things that you consider important. Visualization programs your brain's filter to consider everything relevant to your goal as important. For example, if your goal is to become a world-class public speaker you will begin noticing books about public speaking in a library, advertisements of courses relevant to public speaking in magazines, and videos of great speakers on the internet. You might have seen all this information before, but because you didn't tell your brain's filter that this information is important, it was filtered out. If your brain is the radio, then visualization is a process of tuning the radio on a wave of your goal. After visualization, resources necessary for achieving a goal that you wouldn't notice otherwise will scream from everywhere, as the filter will mark them as worth the attention.

Imagine that your goal is to arrange a two-week family vacation. Firstly, you clearly visualize an ideal vacation in your head. Secondly, you gather information about different vacation options. Thirdly, you generate ideas about how to have the most fun during vacation at the lowest price. Finally, you buy tickets and pack a suitcase. Any achievement in life begins from the first mandatory step – visualization of the dream. Your mental picture serves as a GPS in your brain that directs your actions towards achievement of the goal. Once you have determined what you want, visualize your goal because visualization leads to ideas and enthusiasm, ideas and enthusiasm lead to actions, and actions lead to results. This is one of the most profound principles of success.

Imagination is everything. It is the preview of life's coming attractions. – Albert Einstein, winner, Nobel Prize for Physics

You must first visualize yourself as a success in order to be a success. – Rosa Diaz

If you can see it, and believe it, it is much easier to achieve it. – Oprah Winfrey

Visualization magic formula

Visualization of desire is perhaps the most powerful technique that successful people use to greatly accelerate achievement of their goals. If you tell your brain what you want often enough and clearly enough, it will turn any dream into reality. To achieve goals with 100% guarantee, visualize your ideal future taking into account the magic formula: clarity of visualization X regularity of visualization = achieved goal.

When visualizing a dream, think of a particular moment that sums up everything you associate with successful goal achievement. For example, it could be imagining yourself as the first runner crossing the finish line, imagining yourself receiving congratulations after a job promotion or imagining yourself driving the car of your dreams. Imagine yourself in the middle of the picture and experience a moment of goal achievement by all senses. Imagine what you see, what you hear and what you feel. Keep adding details until you can see a moment of goal achievement clearly. Visualization is perhaps the most powerful tool that successful people use, and its effectiveness directly depends on clarity of your mental picture in which you celebrate and enjoy the achievement of the goal. The more vividly you imagine a moment of goal achievement, the more real it becomes for your subconscious and the more effective visualization is for motivating actions, generating ideas and attracting resources. The more vividly you imagine fulfillment of your dream, the quicker it materializes in the real world.

Goals should be always at the top of your mind to keep the subconscious mind thinking about ideas, to maintain enthusiasm, and to notice necessary resources. The more frequently you visualize your goal as already achieved, the higher the overall impact of visualization on the process of goal achievement and the quicker the picture from your imagination will become reality.

An excellent way to increase the number of times you visualize a goal is to create a dream board. A dream board is a picture or a collection of images that represent what exactly you want to achieve. For example, it could be a picture of your dream car, it could be a picture of a check for $1 million, or a picture of a famous athlete with your head attached to his or her body. You can either draw a picture yourself or create a collage with pictures taken from magazines, newspapers or the internet. Hang your dream board near the desk where you work most of the time, so that you stumble upon it often during the day. The goal of the dream board is to remind you to visualize your goal every time you see it and increase the frequency of your visualizations. Every time you look at your dream board you will think, "Oh, here is my dream. Let's imagine this dream as already fulfilled in the future for a few seconds." With a dream board, you will think about your goal more often and as a result the overall impact of visualization on the process of goal achievement will be higher and you will achieve a goal sooner.

Early in the morning, right after you wake up, and late in the evening, right before you go to bed, are periods of time when visualization is most effective for activating the subconscious mind. Why? When you imagine your goal as achieved before going to sleep, you program your subconscious mind to think during the entire night about ideas that can help to achieve this goal. The subconscious mind works best during the night when the conscious mind is inactive, and if you visualize the goal before going to bed, you will come up with excellent ideas in the morning or later during the day. When you visualize a goal early in the morning you program your subconscious mind to think about ideas that can help to achieve your goal during the entire day. The earlier you first visualize a goal during the day for the first time, the sooner you activate your subconscious mind and the more ideas you will generate during the day that can be helpful to achieve a goal. Make it a habit to visualize goals after waking up and before going to bed because during these time frames activating the subconscious mind is especially powerful.

Visualize your goals frequently and clearly because this is what turns them into reality. Visualization is a magic wand that turns dreams into reality because it motivates actions, stimulates ideas and draws resources. When you work on the goal remember the visualization magic formula: clarity of visualization X frequency of visualization = achieved goal.

The secret to productive goal setting is in establishing clearly defined goals, writing them down and then focusing on them several times a day with words, pictures and emotions as if we've already achieved them. – Denis Waitley

Positive thinking

Law of attraction

Several years ago, I participated in an extreme driving course and one of the techniques I practiced was zigzag driving between obstacles. My instructor said: "Andrii, the car tends to drive towards the point you look at. Don't look at the next obstacle so you don't hit it. Look at the final destination you want to reach instead." The law of attraction says, "You get what you think about most of the time." This law has been used by successful people for thousands of years, it was described in numerous ancient manuscripts and because of its incredible power is often called the law of the universe.

Visualization is incredibly powerful because it instructs your subconscious about which resources to draw, which actions to take and which ideas to generate in order to bring more of what you think about to your life. Your brain will fulfill exactly what you tell it to do and every thought, whether positive or negative, will have an impact on your future. For example if you think, "I don't want to hit this obstacle in the road," you are likely to hit it; however, if you think, "I want to reach the destination safely," you will reach it safely because you draw what you think about. If you think "I have a big debt and it is terrible," you will draw even more financial problems to your life; however, if you think "I want to double my income this year," you will be likely to double it because you draw what you think about. If you think "I am afraid to fail during tomorrow's public presentation," you will be likely to fail; however, if you think "I will make a great presentation tomorrow," you will be likely to make a great presentation because you draw what you think about.

Successful people are extremely solution-oriented and think about how to achieve their dreams most of the time. Unsuccessful people on the contrary think about difficulties, worries and who to blame most of the time. Thoughts become reality, that's why it is important to visualize what you want to achieve rather than what you want to avoid. For example, imagine yourself being fit and healthy rather than worry about your extra weight. Take control of what you think about because your subconscious works as a thought amplifier and will ultimately turn into reality what you think about most of the time, whether it is something good or something bad.

Results you are experiencing in your life today are a reflection of thoughts you had yesterday. Change the balance between positive and negative thoughts in your head, and you will live the life of your dreams. How? Make a conscious decision to feed your brain with positive thoughts and to block negative thoughts.

Put your brain on a positive diet

Wear positive glasses

Imagine that you have won in a lottery and bought the car of your dreams. In the morning, you notice that somebody has scratched it in a parking lot. Although almost everything in your life is awesome, you might concentrate the majority of your time on a single bad thing – a scratch. When people have 99% good things and 1% bad things in their life they concentrate their attention on exactly 1% bad things. Because we get what we think about, these thoughts attract even more negative events in their lives and block everything that is good. The happiness and greatness of your future depends on your ability to concentrate your attention on the 99% good things in your life and to be happy about what you already have.

If you concentrate your attention on the 1% negative things in your life, you will draw negative events. If you think about and appreciate the 99% good things, you will draw positive events. You will get and achieve anything you want, once you learn to appreciate life. Be happy about everything you already have, about all the little things that surround you without any specific reason. "I am alive. And I am happy about it," "I have a computer and I am happy about it," "The sun is shining – awesome," "I will have lunch soon. Cool!" At first, you smile and think positively about the little good things that surround you deliberately and later this positive energy will draw everything you want. Successful people concentrate most of their time on what is good in their lives rather than what is bad in their lives.

Whether you expect bad things to happen in your life or good things to happen in your life, you will rarely be disappointed because we draw what we think about. Successful people always expect that something good will happen to them. Their attitude is: "The world is friendly to me. The world is full of resources and supports me on the way to my goals." Positive expectations of successful people according to the law of attraction draw necessary resources, ideas and events that help them to achieve their goals.

Focus your attention on things that are currently good in your life. Expect that great things will happen in your life in the future. Wearing positive glasses and being an optimist will significantly improve your positive and negative thoughts balance, which will draw happiness and success to your life. Behind your habit of seeing life through the positive lens lies success in all aspects of life: money, relationships, health and personal development.

Feed your brain with positive thoughts

Every thought, whether positive or negative, that comes to your mind will impact your life. Since we get what we think about most of the time, in order to change the ratio of positive to negative thoughts and draw success, deposit positive thoughts into your mind intentionally. Simply say to yourself regularly positive assertive statements about anything you want to be true and your performance and success will skyrocket.

For example, once you wake up you may think, "I will enjoy every minute of this day and it may be the best day of my life." During the day you can say to yourself, "I am drawing a huge amount of resources and ideas," "I am financially free and have as much money as I need," "I am a magnet for success and luck," "I am brimming with energy and am overflowing with joy," or "I possess the qualities needed to be extremely successful." Before going to bed you might say, "Creative energy surges through me and leads me to new and brilliant ideas," "I am happy about myself," and "Tomorrow I will have a very successful day."

Once you increase the number of positive thoughts that flow through your brain daily, you will draw ideas, resources and events that will help to make your dreams a reality. Once you increase the number of positive thoughts that flow through your brain daily, you will be energetic, cheerful and charismatic. Once you increase the number of positive thoughts that flow through your brain daily, you will become a happier person. As we draw what we think about most of the time, the nature of your dominant thoughts is a root cause of your success or failure. Being an optimist is lucrative because positive thinking brings much more success in life than negative thinking.

Glaring Sphere Technique

Glaring Sphere is an excellent technique that can amplify the power of positive thoughts and fill you with necessary energy for achievement of goals. Glaring Sphere is an excellent technique to do during "wasted time" such as taking a shower, waiting in line, jogging or walking to the parking lot. Glaring Sphere is one of the most powerful techniques in success psychology and I am sure it will bring you great results as it has brought to thousands of people worldwide

Tell yourself several positive statements that you want to be true. For example, "I attract money like a magnet," "I am incredibly successful," and "I am generating successful business ideas." Simultaneously imagine a little glaring sphere inside you that is full of qualities mentioned in the positive statements. In our example, the glaring sphere would be full of money magnetism, successfulness and creativity. In your mental picture, simultaneously increase the glare of the sphere and the concentration of qualities mentioned in the positive statements. Imagine how the sphere grows in size until it covers your entire body, then how it grows until it covers the entire room, then the entire city and finally the entire planet. After you clearly see a mental image of the glaring sphere full of qualities mentioned in the positive statements with a center inside you that covers the entire planet, the exercise is finished. Your subconscious clearly received your message and will do everything to draw what you want as much as possible to your life.

The Glaring Sphere technique allows you to at least mentally become a superman or a super woman and to gain qualities you need to achieve your dreams. And you know what the coolest part is? You can choose whatever qualities you want.

The following chain reaction occurs in our life: If you experience positive emotions today, they will create your tomorrow and tomorrow you will also experience positive emotions; if you experience positive emotions tomorrow, they will build your day after tomorrow and the day after tomorrow you will also experience positive emotions. Make yourself a rule to intentionally create positive emotions in your life by concentrating attention on positive things, expecting positive events to happen in the future and feeding your brain with positive thoughts. This habit will allow you to get into the flow of positive events and to make each subsequent day more joyful than the previous one.

Eliminate negative thoughts

Block negative thoughts

Your subconscious mind is programmed by your thoughts and is incredibly powerful in drawing what you think about most of the time to your life. However, with great power comes a great responsibility because the subconscious mind not only can bring good things to your life and make it happy, but also bring bad things to your life and make it miserable. Your brain will fulfill exactly what you tell it to do and every thought whether positive or negative will have an impact on your future.

For example, if you are trying to create a business and the following thoughts come to your mind, "I am not cut out for this," "I doubt it is possible," or "I am worth nothing," these negative thoughts will block your subconscious from generating ideas, will reduce your enthusiasm to take action, will prevent you from noticing valuable resources and at the first sign of difficulty you will throw a white flag and say to yourself: "You see, I was right when I said that I am not cut out for this, it's not possible and I am worth nothing." Every thought serves as a command for your subconscious to turn this thought into reality. If you think that you are poor, you are likely to become poorer, if you fear being fired you increase your chances of getting fired, if you doubt that you can achieve your goal, you become less likely to achieve it. Negative thoughts draw negative events and if they constitute the majority of thoughts in your head, they can literally make your life miserable. You might ask, "How can I protect myself from the negative thoughts then?"

Firstly, control thoughts that get into your head and once you notice that a particular thought is negative, for example, "I am poor," "I am unlucky," or "I don't have time," consciously block it. Tell yourself: "I won't let this thought poison my subconscious and make my life less awesome than it can be." Secondly, when you hear other people around you being pessimistic and discussing how something is bad or impossible, either avoid communicating with them or change the topic of the conversation. Negative thoughts that you hear from other people are toxic and dangerous poison because they can affect your own thoughts and results in life. Reduce the amount of negative thoughts that you hear from other people in private conversations, reduce the amount of negative thoughts that you hear from other people on TV, and reduce the amount of negative thoughts that you hear from other people on the internet.

Positive people have positive expectations in their lives and most of their days are successful. Negative people have negative expectations in their lives and most of their days are unsuccessful. By reducing the amount of negative thoughts that flow through your head, you can significantly improve your results in life. Enjoy your life today, only so you can make it even more awesome in the future.

React positively to both positive and negative events

Imagine that a colleague at work stole your wallet. After you had a conversation with your manager and the robber the wallet was returned. Despite a good end to the incident, you stay angry at the colleague for 2 more months and every negative thought that comes to your mind draws unpleasant events to your life. A bad event in your life isn't as dangerous as the flow of negative thoughts that it can activate in your head. It's the negative thoughts that make us unhappy and bring harm to ourselves, not the events.

The majority of people are used to reacting with positive thoughts to positive events and with negative thoughts to negative events. Once you develop a habit to react positively to both positive and negative events, you will get into the fast lane towards the life of your dreams because we draw what we think about most of the time. You might think, "How is it possible to react positively to negative events?"

Firstly, when people do bad things to you, always forgive them instantly and say to yourself, "I forgive this person and wish him or her well." Of course, you can take actions to prevent these people from doing bad things to you again or avoid communicating with them in the future, but you need to forgive them quickly to stop a flow of negative and destructive thoughts that may affect your future. When you forgive people it's not they who benefit, it's you who benefits.

Secondly, find something positive in every negative event and develop a mindset that everything that happens in your life can help you to fulfill your dreams in one way or another. For example: You failed in business – "That's OK, I learned a valuable lesson and will act better next time." You need to wait for 10 hours at the airport – "Excellent! I will have time to read an interesting book." Somebody swears at you – "I enjoy life, appreciate that most people around me don't swear and wish this person well."

Sure, unpleasant things that are out of your control occasionally happen, but there's one thing you always have control over – your reaction. If you think negatively about negative events you draw even more bad things to your life. Make a conscious decision to react positively to all negative events because of the following benefits: maintaining high self-confidence and motivation to take actions, programming your subconscious mind to think about solutions rather than problems and drawing good events. This decision can reduce the number of unpleasant experiences in your life to a minimum and make you incredibly successful in achievement of your goals.

Don't take opinions of other people to heart

When people hear about your goal and say, "It's impossible," "It's unrealistic," or "Here are ten reasons why it can't be achieved," thank them for their opinion, calculate the risks and never think about this feedback again. If you become really concerned about somebody saying "You can't," you will activate a flow of negative thoughts in your head which will block creativity, lower motivation, draw failures and eventually bury your dream. If having everyone believe in your idea was a requirement for success then nobody would ever be able to achieve anything. Even the most successful ideas in the world such as the telephone, radio and The Beatles band initially received negative feedback.

Associates of David Sarnoff replied to his request to invest in radio in 1921: "The wireless music box has no imaginable commercial value. Who would pay for a message sent to no one in particular?"

After the audition by The Beatles, the Decca Records executive gave his verdict to the band's manager: "Not to mince words, Mr. Epstein, but we don't like your boys' sound. Groups are out; four-piece groups with guitars particularly are finished."

Western Union officials who reviewed Alexander Graham Bell's offer to purchase his telephone patent wrote: "The Telephone purports to transmit the speaking voice over telegraph wires. We found that the voice is very weak and indistinct, and grows even weaker when long wires are used between the transmitter and receiver. Technically, we do not see that this device will ever be capable of sending recognizable speech over a distance of several miles. Messrs. Hubbard and Bell want to install one of their 'telephone devices' in every city. The idea is idiotic on the face of it. Furthermore, why would any person want to use this ungainly and impractical device when he can send a messenger to the telegraph office and have a clear written message sent to any large city in the United States?"

Negative opinions of people can't bury your dream, but your reaction to them can. Whenever you hear "You can't," thank the person for his or her opinion, calculate the risks and never think about it again because a flow of negative thoughts activated by your internal critic can be detrimental to your success.

Life is 10% what happens to you and 90% how you react to it. – Charles R. Swindoll

You have to believe in yourself when no one else does. That's what makes you a winner. – Venus Williams, Olympic gold medalist and professional tennis champion

Strategy

A plan for achieving a goal

According to research by psychology professor Dr. Gail Matthews at Dominican University, people who just think about their goals achieve them with 43% probability. People who not only think about their goals but also write down their goals achieve them with 61% probability. But people who in addition to writing down goals, also create a plan with specific action items and regularly check progress, increase their chances for success to 76%. Of course these numbers may be different depending on circumstances and the nature of your goal, but one thing is certain: having a plan with clear action items is critical for making your dreams a reality.

If you develop a plan on how to achieve a goal, you create a map in your brain that shows the way towards the goal. With the map all actions you take will be aligned in the direction to the goal, and their individual positive effects will be combined. After you have clearly decided what goal you want to achieve and have written it down, develop an action plan.

Many years ago I asked a serial entrepreneur, multimillionaire and exceptional goal-achiever, "Jason, imagine that you want to launch a new business. How would you decide which actions to take first?" He replied, "Andrii, if I wake up in the morning and decide to become a chocolate producer, I break this complex task into several simpler ones: 'How can I produce tasty chocolates?' and 'How can I sell many chocolates?'

"Each of these problems I split into several even smaller problems. 'How can I produce tasty chocolates?' may be split into: 'How do I get a recipe for tasty chocolate?' and 'How do I outsource production of my chocolate?' The task, 'How can I sell many chocolates?' may be split into: 'How can I sell chocolates through supermarkets?' and 'How can I promote chocolates through media?'

"All tasks get split into smaller tasks until they get so small that by thinking about them, I can come to specific actions that need to be taken.

"I use this strategy every day for solving complex business tasks. Andrii, if you want to solve a complex problem, just build a pyramid from smaller problems and you will be able to solve tasks that seem unsolvable from the first glance."

To develop an action plan regularly ask yourself, "How can I achieve my goal?" or "What else can I do to make my dream a reality?" These questions will stimulate your subconscious mind to generate ideas of how to split achieving your big goal into sub goals and which particular action steps need to be taken to accomplish each of them. Write all ideas for action steps that you generate and consider valuable into the action plan. After you began a journey towards the goal, regularly update your plan taking into account new ideas you generate, obstacles you face and results you get because the best strategy is a flexible strategy.

For example, imagine that your goal is to be able to do 100 pull-ups at a time. You ask yourself, "How can I achieve my goal?" and get two ideas for the initial plan: "I need to install a bar at home" and "I need to find a training plan recommended by a person who can do more than 100 pull-ups." In 3 weeks, you increased the number of pull-ups that you can do but realized that you stopped making progress. You ask yourself, "What else can I do to make my dream a reality?" and update your plan with new ideas, "I need to switch the training plan to a more effective one" and "I need to also add pushups to my training that develop chest muscles necessary for pull-ups."

When, as a college student, I first went to the gym, I noticed guys who were carrying with them everywhere a paper with their workout plan. I thought, "Why do they bother writing this plan and don't just do random fitness exercises like me?" In a few months I realized that the guys with the best results in the gym were always these guys who carried a plan.

After you have clearly decided what you want and have written down your dream, create a plan with specific action items. Regularly measure your progress and based on the lessons you learn on the way to the goal and the results you achieve, update the plan. Developing a plan and regularly improving it is one of most important concepts that successful people use for achieving their goals.

Measure progress

In order to increase the effectiveness of the effort you make towards achieving a goal, measure progress regularly. There are two reasons why measuring progress is important.

Firstly, progress is one of the best motivators in the world to take action, and the best way to recognize the progress towards the goal is to measure it. Imagine that you want to lose weight and begin weighing yourself every morning. When you stand on the scale and see the number that is lower than the one you saw yesterday, you experience a small success. When you experience success, dopamine, a happiness-inducing hormone, is released in the brain and as a result you feel joy. Guess what? You will do your best to eat less during the day and to exercise to experience joy from progress again. Regular progress measurement and intermediate celebrations will help you to not only achieve a goal but enjoy a process of achieving it.

Secondly, regular progress measurement week by week, day by day, or hour by hour will allow you to quickly identify where you are not progressing as you wanted. Successful people always know exactly where they are on the way to their goal and once they see that what they do hasn't been bringing them closer to the goal for a while, they quickly adjust their strategy.

To achieve a goal of any size you need to make measurable progress towards it every day. Measuring progress will allow you to stay motivated to take actions in the direction of the goal and know when you need to change a strategy if your progress stops or slows down. Decide whether to measure a progress by means of checklists, percentages, pounds, pages, dollars or any other means, and also which intermediate points you should go through on the way to the destination.

What's measured improves. — Peter F. Drucker

A perfect strategy is a flexible strategy

A famous French naturalist, Jean-Henri Fabre, conducted an interesting experiment with Pine Processionary caterpillars. He took several caterpillars and placed them in single file around the rim of a flowerpot. Each caterpillar's head touched the end of the caterpillar in front of it so that the procession formed a full circle. Fabre placed pine needles, which are the favorite food of the caterpillars of this type, in the middle of the circle formed by the procession. What makes a Processionary caterpillar special is the instinct to blindly follow the caterpillar in front of it. All caterpillars went in circles hour after hour, day after day, night after night thinking that the caterpillar in front of them was heading to the food. In 7 days, all the caterpillars died from hunger and exhaustion although food was just 6 inches away from them and the only thing they needed to do to get it was to change the direction of movement. The procession died simply because when the strategy of finding food didn't give results, the caterpillars didn't change it.

Millions of people who fail to achieve their goals follow the principle "It was always done here this way." Just like Processionary caterpillars, they do something actively every day, don't get results, but instead of changing their strategy continue doing what they were doing.

If you want to achieve your goal, the strategy you are using need not be clever or original but it should bring results. If you see that what you are doing isn't bringing results, simply change your approach. If that approach again doesn't produce results, keep changing it until what you do brings you closer to your goal.

Successful people know that the perfect strategy to achieve a goal is a flexible strategy that is constantly adjusted based on the results it brings. Do more of what works, do less of what doesn't and experiment to see if you can make your strategy even more effective. When you take actions in the direction of your desires, analyze your actions, improve your actions and change your actions, you will never stop making progress towards the life of your dreams.

For every failure, there's an alternative course of action. You just have to find it. When you come to a roadblock, take a detour. – Mary Kay Ash, founder of Mary Kay Cosmetics

When I was young I thought that people at the top really understood what the hell was happening ... whether they were cardinals or bishops or generals or politicians or business leaders. They knew. Well, I'm up there, and now I know they don't know. – David Mahoney

One step closer to the goal

In 1977, at the age of only 18, Terry Fox was diagnosed with bone cancer and his right leg was amputated 6 inches above the knee. While staying at a hospital, Terry was so touched by the suffering of other patients (many of them young children) that he decided to run across Canada to raise money for cancer research. Within 143 days, Terry ran 3,339 miles across Canada with prosthesis at a rate of almost 26 miles per day. When asked how he managed to cover such an enormous distance, he said: "I just keep running to the next telephone pole."

If you think about the amount of work that needs to be done to achieve a big goal, you may be scared even to begin. No matter how big your goal is, it is always achieved one step, one task and one measure at a time. If you always focus only on the next step that can get you closer to the goal, and make a little bit of progress every day, you will definitely achieve your dream. After you achieve it and look back on what you have accomplished, you will be amazed and proud of yourself.

Imagine that you are driving a car in a thick fog and can see only 10 yards in front of you. After you pass these 10 yards, you see the next 10 yards, and after you pass them yet another 10 yards. You don't see the entire way but by concentrating on the next 10 yards at each point in time, you will be able to cover any distance to your destination.

Often people have a dream but are afraid to start because they don't see the path completely and the outcome is uncertain. Achieving a big goal is often similar to driving in a thick fog because when you move towards your goal, you don't need to know the entire way but you just need to know how to take the next step. Once you have taken a step, you will see how to take a consequent step and if you keep moving you will eventually reach the destination.

No matter how huge your goal is and how unclear the path is that leads to it, you will always get from where you are to where you want to be if you focus on taking just one next step. Take this step, then a logical next step, and then yet another step and eventually you will realize that your dream becomes a reality. Ask yourself, "What can I do today to get at least one step closer to my dream?" and remember that an elephant is eaten one piece at a time.

The Idea Lifestyle Bundle

How to run an ultramarathon? Puff out your chest, put one foot in front of the other, and don't stop till you cross the finish line. — Dean Karnazes

A journey of a thousand leagues begins with a single step. — Lao Tzu

You don't try to build a wall. You don't set out to build a wall. You don't say, 'I'm going to build the biggest, baddest, greatest wall that's ever been built.' You don't start there. You say, 'I'm going to lay this brick as perfectly as a brick can be laid.' And then you do that every single day, and soon you have a wall. — Will Smith

Take massive action towards the goal

Law of inertia

During the winter when I was 12, I missed 2 weeks of ballroom dance classes due to illness. After I recovered and was supposed to go to the upcoming dance class, I realized that it was rather difficult to do. I thought, "I am a bit lazy today. I just don't feel like turning off the TV and going outside from the cozy apartment. I will miss just one more class." In a few days, just 15 minutes before I had to go to the dance school, I realized, "I am still lazy and don't want to go outside. If it requires so much effort to just leave the apartment today, how much effort it will require me to attend the dance school regularly?"

That day, I finally summoned up my willpower and forced myself to get out of the apartment. After the class I realized, "Wow! I enjoyed all 1.5 hours of the class. I learned 3 new movements and I feel very energetic. How awesome it is that I finally went to the class. I love dancing!" After that day I attended the dance school regularly again, it didn't take me any effort or willpower to get out of the apartment and I never missed a class before the summer break. After the summer break in September, just before going to the first dance class of the school year, I realized that it was rather difficult to do. I thought, "I am a bit lazy today. If I miss just one class it probably won't be a big deal." I learned that if I attend dance classes regularly it's easy and enjoyable to continue attending them, but if I miss several classes in a row it requires a huge effort to begin attending them again.

Newton's Law of Motion or Law of Inertia says, "An object at rest stays at rest and an object in motion stays in motion with the same speed and in the same direction <u>unless acted upon by an unbalanced force.</u>" What this law essentially says is that it takes much less effort to maintain motion than to begin motion from a state of rest.

For example, a car consumes much more fuel to begin movement than to maintain movement, that's why fuel consumption in a traffic jam is higher than on a highway. Although Newton originally stated his law for physical movement, it also very well applies to movement towards our goals. Just like a car, you spend much more energy to take a first step towards your goal than to keep moving towards the goal.

"Many people think, if I feel so lazy to even begin taking action, how miserable it will be to go through the entire way to the goal?" Actually, on the way to the goal over 50% of effort is spent to just take a first step in its direction. Once you take the first step no matter how small and build a momentum, it will be easy for you to maintain movement towards the goal.

If you want to learn how to dance, go to the dance school and attend the first class. If you want to start a business, generate 100 business ideas during the brainstorming session. If you want to travel around the world, choose an exact route and estimate the cost. One of the most important things in achieving any goal is just to begin.

In numerous studies, psychologists have observed that people have a tendency to feel discomfort if they have started the task, but not finished it, the so-called Zeigarnik effect. In one research study, participants were given "brain buster" tasks and were interrupted before they could complete them. Although the participants were told to stop, nearly 90% of them finished the task anyway. Due to the Law of Inertia, people tend to procrastinate to take the first step towards their goals, but once it's taken they tend to finish what they have started because if they don't, due to the Zeigarnik effect they will experience discomfort.

Remember that if you want to achieve a goal, your main task is to simply take a first step. One step, no matter how small, may be enough to keep you moving towards the goal and make sure you don't stop until you achieve it.

You don't have to be great to get started, but you have to get started to be great. – Les Brown

Take massive directed action now

A few years ago, I met a highly successful entrepreneur and millionaire named John. John shared with me the following story: "When I was a student, I wanted very much to become a sales associate to earn my first paycheck. I went into the shopping mall, walked along the line of the apparel boutiques, entered each of them and asked, 'Who can I talk to about a job as a sales associate? Do you need a sales associate?' At the third boutique that I entered, a manager asked, 'Where did you see our job advertisement?' I smiled and said, 'I was just walking along the line of apparel boutiques, and decided to ask if you have an opening.' Although my approach surprised the manager, he interviewed me immediately. In half an hour I had a second interview with a senior manager and eventually received a job offer. Between the time I entered the shopping mall and the time I got a job, three hours elapsed. Had I known that I should write a résumé, prepare for the interview and have previous sales experience, my job search would have probably taken much, much longer."

Successful people know that the only thing you have control over is your own actions and to achieve a goal you need to take massive action. The more actions you take and the more seeds you plant, the bigger crop of results you will eventually gather and the sooner you will achieve your goal. Successful people are extremely action-oriented. Rather than spending excessive time on developing a plan and talking, they take a plunge, take massive action and correct their strategy along the way.

People often say, "I haven't taken a first step towards my goal because I am waiting for more favorable circumstances" or "I am waiting until I have more money" or "I am waiting until I get a better education." Remember that the perfect time to achieve your biggest goal is right now. The perfect resources to achieve the goal are those you have today. Instead of planning too long, thinking too long or waiting for the most favorable circumstances, take the first step towards the goal right now. You will realize that new opportunities, ideas and resources come to you not while you are waiting for them, but while you are taking actions towards the goal.

Be truthful to yourself: nothing will happen on its own, nobody will pull you anywhere, and complaints never help. If you want to get warmth from the oven you need to constantly feed it with firewood. Life works exactly like an oven, you first need to take action before you can see the results and experience joy, and to see a lot of results and experience a lot of joy regularly you need to take massive action daily. The amount of action you take is correlated with the progress you make, the amount of goals you achieve and the joy you experience.

The only thing that can make your life better is your own actions. The sooner you take a first step and the more actions you take regularly, the faster you will drive on the highway towards the life of your dreams.

Too many people spend too much time trying to perfect something before they actually do it. Instead of waiting for perfection, run with what you got, and fix it along the way. – Paul Arden

The one requirement for success in our business lives is effort. Either you make the commitment to get results or you don't. – Mark Cuban

Talent is cheaper than table salt. What separates the talented individual from the successful one is a lot of hard work. – Stephen King

Focus attention

What you focus your attention on is where your energy flows and what eventually gets done. Once you focus your attention on the goal, your mind generates ideas relevant to this goal and you take actions relevant to this goal. If you focus your attention on something else, you think about something else and take actions relevant to something else.

We always make choices of where to focus our attention and if you think about the past, you will notice that the most successful areas of your life are those where you have focused your attention the most. What gets your attention is eventually done. If you focus your attention on jogging, you jog. If you focus your attention on a phone conversation, you talk. If you focus your attention on your business, you generate business ideas or take actions that will develop it.

If you are not moving closer to your goal or your progress is slow, it simply means that you have decided to focus your attention elsewhere. In order to live the life of your dreams and fulfill your desires, you need to take necessary actions, and in order to take them you first need to focus your attention on your desires and the longer the better. If you make a conscious decision to focus attention as much as possible on the goal, you will take more necessary actions, generate more necessary ideas and achieve it sooner.

The American Journal of Experimental Psychology reported a study in which students spent approximately 40% longer on solving difficult math problems if they had to occasionally switch to other tasks. Another study done by Gloria Mark, an "interruption scientist" at the University of California, revealed that people who often switch between tasks work faster, but less productively. Both these studies showed that people who multitask not only are less productive than those who work on a single task at a time, but also experience a significantly higher level of stress, frustration and workload.

Very often if you recall how your day was spent, you might say, "I drank coffee, talked to a colleague, watched videos on the Internet, checked emails, read the news, talked on the phone and worked in between." All these distracters not only reduce the time you work during the day, but also make you much less productive during the time you actually work because as studies show, work with interruptions is less productive than work without interruptions.

How can you increase productivity and reduce the amount of stress while you take actions necessary to achieve your goal? Cut out all distracters such as social networks, phone calls or instant messaging and focus your attention completely on a single task for 30, 45 or 60 minutes without interruption, so that your entire energy is directed at it. When you dive into the task, forget about what happens around you and about all other activities, you will be much more productive. This state of focus, involvement and concentration gives hyper results. If you stop multitasking and practice single tasking, you will not only become significantly more productive but will also have much less stress in your life.

In order to achieve a goal you need to take actions. If you consciously decide to focus your attention on your goal as much as possible, it will guarantee that you take enough actions and will eventually achieve the goal. To make the time that you spend working towards the goal most productive and enjoyable, concentrate on a single task for 30, 45 or 60 minutes with minimum amount of interruptions.

My success is due more to my ability to work continuously on one thing without stopping than to any other single quality. – Thomas Edison

I've learned that only through focus can you do world-class things, no matter how capable you are. – Bill Gates

Concentrate all your thoughts upon the work at hand. The sun's rays do not burn until brought to a focus. – Alexander Graham Bell

Set a deadline

Two days before an exam, college students are perhaps the most productive people in the world. They cut out all entertainment, phone calls, social networks and focus entirely on exam preparation. Before the exam, they often study more than 16 hours per day with extremely high productivity. Why does this happen? They think, "I have a very strict deadline that is very close. I really want to pass the exam and I have no other options than to prepare within just two days." The reason for students' super-productivity is the deadlines.

Deadlines develop a sense of urgency and make your internal voice periodically say, "The deadline you have to meet is close. Focus your attention and energy entirely on the goal. Take action without procrastination." Deadlines force your subconscious mind to generate ideas more effectively. Deadlines are the tool that allows you to increase attention, focus on the task you want to accomplish and achieve more goals in less time.

For each goal you want to achieve, even if you don't know exactly how you will achieve it, set a firm deadline. For example, "I will be able to do 25 pull-ups by October 21" or "I will create a website for my company within 2 months." Once you begin moving in the direction of the goal and learn new information, you may adjust the deadline if necessary.

In order for the deadline to help you to increase productivity, make sure that it is realistic in your mind however with a stretch. For example, if you decide to lose 20 pounds in 2 days, you won't believe that you can do that and won't take any action at all to achieve this goal. If you decide to lose 20 pounds in 10 years, you will procrastinate taking any actions because the deadline is very far away. However, if you decide to lose 20 pounds in 3 months, you will believe that it is possible and also have a sense of urgency to take action right now in order to meet the deadline.

You might reasonably ask, "What should I do if I don't meet the deadline?" Of course if you miss the deadline, you shouldn't stop pursuing your goal, but just set a new deadline and continue working on the goal until you achieve it. Make sure that for each goal and sub goal you set a realistic deadline, however with a stretch that will create an internal pressure to take massive action without procrastination and to do your best to achieve a goal as quickly as possible. This technique gives hyper results in little time.

Failures and persistence

Failures are your friends

In order to become a great dancer you first need to do a movement incorrectly, then correct yourself and improve your movement. In order to become a great violin player you first need to play a composition incorrectly, then correct yourself and play it better the next time. In order to become a successful entrepreneur you first need to fail, learn why what you did didn't work out and then change your approach. High achievers know that in order to achieve a goal, you need to make good decisions. Good decisions come from experience and experience comes from failures. When you fail, you learn what doesn't work and why. This experience is the reason why you eventually succeed.

Professor Dean Keith decided to explore the relationship between the quantity and quality of ideas. He studied the work of hundreds of the most creative scientists and made a very interesting discovery. The best scientists created more successful ideas than the mediocre ones. However, the best scientists also created many more bad ideas than the mediocre scientists.

The vast majority of papers written by the world's most famous scientists were never cited. A small percentage of them received a little over 100 citations and only several papers had an incredible impact on the world. Professor Keith has done the same study with composers and other fine artists and found that the more bad ideas a composer, a scientist or an artist generated, the more successful ideas he or she had.

Thomas Edison filed over 2,000 patents, but the majority of them didn't make him a cent. Albert Einstein published over 300 scientific papers, but the majority of them are not cited by other scientists. Pablo Picasso created more than 20,000 pieces of art, but most of them are not presented at the best art exhibitions. There is a direct correlation between quantity and quality of ideas. The majority of ideas that the best idea creators generate are bad, some of them are average and very few are genius. These few genius ideas make the best creators enormously successful.

When Walt Disney was seeking funding for Disneyland in Anaheim, California, he was rejected by 302 bankers before he received the necessary funding. James Dyson created 5,126 failed prototypes before creating a working version of a dual-cyclone bagless vacuum cleaner. R.H. Macy started seven failed businesses before finally creating Macy's department store in New York City and making billions of dollars.

Successful people fail far more often than other people and the size of their success is proportional to the number of failures they make. Successful people are hungry for failures because they know that the more they fail, the more they learn, the more they learn, the better they act, and the better they act, the sooner they succeed. Perceive failures as an essential component of success and instead of being scared of failures, double your failure rate because a life without failures is a life without achievement and a life without achievement is a life without happiness.

It doesn't matter how many times you fail. It doesn't matter how many times you almost get it right. No one is going to know or care about your failures, and neither should you. All you have to do is learn from them and those around you because… All that matters in business is that you get it right once. Then everyone can tell you how lucky you are. – Mark Cuban

Unless you're not pushing yourself, you're not living to the fullest. You can't be afraid to fail, but unless you fail, you haven't pushed hard enough. – Dean Karnazes

The person interested in success has to learn to view failure as a healthy, inevitable part of the process getting to the top. – Dr. Joyce Brothers

Life's persistence test

In 1867 one of the best engineers of his time, John Roebling, decided to build a spectacular suspension bridge that would connect Brooklyn with Manhattan in New York. As there was no bridge of such magnitude ever built before, engineers around the world said, "Building a bridge of this type is impossible. Forget this idea." Despite the opinions of colleagues, John Roebling wholeheartedly believed that he could build the bridge of his dreams. The only person who shared John's vision was his son Washington, who at that time was an upcoming engineer. Together they created a detailed plan, hired a crew and started working on the bridge with a lot of enthusiasm.

A few months after a tragic accident at the site in 1869, John died and Washington took charge of the entire project. Fate was so cruel that shortly after Washington took charge of the bridge, as a result of construction-related decompression sickness, his body was completely paralyzed. He wasn't able to walk or talk and the only body part that he could move was one finger. The experts who said before the project started that building a bridge of this type was impossible now said, "Remember how we said that starting this project was totally unreasonable? John and Washington Roebling are crazy fools!"

Most people would certainly give up at this point but Washington, although handicapped, was determined to accomplish building the bridge, even though he didn't know how yet. One day an idea came to Washington while he was lying on his hospital bed: "Hey, the only thing I can do is move one finger. I will develop a code to communicate with my wife by moving a single finger!"

Thus Washington developed a code that allowed him to communicate with his wife, Emily, by tapping with his finger on her arm. For 13 years, Emily interpreted Washington's instructions for engineers and helped to supervise the construction until the bridge was finally completed in 1883. Whenever you are pursuing your dream and a thought of "Should I give up or should I persist?" comes to your mind, remember the story of the Brooklyn Bridge, the bridge that was built by one finger.

People often blame external circumstances and obstacles for their inactivity. The Brooklyn Bridge story demonstrates that no matter what the circumstances are, if you persist you will always achieve your goal. The external circumstances can't stop you, the only thing that can stop you is the limitations you create in your head, yourself. Obstacles are as essential a part of the process of fulfilling dreams as rain is an essential part of the weather. When rain starts you don't blame the rain, but simply pull out an umbrella; when you face an obstacle don't blame the obstacle but just constructively look for a way to overcome it.

Successful people fall down, pick themselves up and try again, over and over again before they pass life's "persistence test" and achieve what they want. Thomas Edison once said: "When I have fully decided that a result is worth getting, I go ahead of it and make trial after trial until it comes. Nearly every man, who develops an idea, works it up to the point where it looks impossible, and then gets discouraged. That's not the place to become discouraged." Remember that success is a game of character and defeat is not possible as long as you don't stop trying to achieve a goal and continue to move forward.

History has demonstrated that the most notable winners usually encountered heartbreaking obstacles before they triumphed. They won because they refused to become discouraged by their defeats. – B.C. Forbes, founder of Forbes magazine

I can summarize the lessons of my life in seven words – never give in; never, never give in. – Winston Churchill

I do not think there is any other quality so essential to success of any kind, as the quality of perseverance. It overcomes almost everything, even nature. – John D. Rockefeller, at one time the richest self-made man in the world

The difference in winning and losing is most often, not quitting. – Walt Disney

Fuel for achieving goals

Burning desire to achieve a goal

In 1979 James Dyson bought one of the most advanced vacuum cleaners on the market, and after using it got frustrated with how quickly it clogged and began losing suction. James got excited about this problem and decided, "I will design a vacuum cleaner that will clean the house more effectively."

Partly supported by the salary of his wife, who worked as an art teacher, and partly by bank loans, James spent almost 5 years working on his vacuum cleaner design and after 5,126 failed prototypes eventually created a working version of a dual-cyclone bagless vacuum cleaner. In a few years, the Dyson vacuum cleaner became one of the most desirable household appliances worldwide and James Dyson became a billionaire.

People often wonder about persistence of successful people and their ability to overcome obstacles. When you want to drive from point A to point B you need enough fuel in the tank. No matter how powerful your car is, without enough fuel you will never reach your destination. The same is true with goal setting. If you want to fulfill your desire, you need to have enough motivation inside, or you will never reach it.

What motivated James Dyson to continue working on the bagless vacuum cleaner after 5,000 failed prototypes? What motivated Walt Disney to pursue his dream after 300 banks refused to give him a loan for building Disneyland? What motivated Agatha Christie to continue writing after 5 years of rejections from publishing houses?

At an early age, children are taught to use PUSH motivation to achieve goals. PUSH motivation is when you take action because of your discipline, willpower or fear of punishment. In childhood, we get most of our goals from adults. A teacher says, "Do your homework," parents say, "Clean your room," a trainer says, "Do 10 pull-ups." You think, "I don't want to do my homework (or clean my room or do 10 pull-ups) but I will PUSH myself and do it." PUSH motivation works well for small short-term goals that are set in front of you by somebody else. However, PUSH motivation doesn't last long and doesn't bring big results. When people grow up and set their own goals they, out of habit, often continue to use PUSH motivation. The use of PUSH motivation is the biggest reason why people fail to achieve goals and to live the lives of their dreams.

The reason why James Dyson, Walt Disney, Agatha Christie and millions of other people achieved their goals is that they used the motivation of DESIRE. Motivation of DESIRE is when you take actions not because of fear, not because you have a strong willpower or discipline but because you have a burning desire to achieve a goal and this motivation is thousands times more powerful than PUSH motivation.

In order to achieve amazing goals, you need a lot of energy and your burning desire is the source of this energy. The amount of this energy is proportional to the intensity of desire. The bigger the goal you want to achieve, the more intense your desire should be to get from where you are to where you want to be. Burning desire is the huge power that will give you energy to complete the necessary work, overcome obstacles and endure failures on the way to the goal.

When you have a burning desire to achieve a goal, you feel goose bumps even by thinking about your future. When you have a burning desire to achieve a goal, you feel as if a part of you is dying if you are not pursuing it. When you have a burning desire, you wake up in the morning excited to take a couple of more steps in the direction of the goal.

People who don't have enough motivation are likely to give up once they face the first difficulties on the way to the goal. But when you want something very, very, very much, the conversation that happens in your head usually sounds like, "Hey, I feel miserable after failure. Maybe quitting is a good option? But I very much want to create this vacuum cleaner." "Maybe, let's do something less stressful, this goal is not for you? But I want to create this vacuum cleaner very much, and won't feel OK unless I achieve it. Maybe postpone it for better times? But I want it very much."

I noticed that if I wanted something really badly I always got it. There was not a single situation in my life, my wife's life, my students' lives and the lives of people I ever had a conversation with when we wanted something really badly and didn't get it. Do you know why this happens? It happens because the power of motivation of DESIRE is so huge, that no matter how unachievable the goal seems, it will get you to your destination guaranteed.

When you want something but still don't have it then you either don't really want it, or don't want it badly enough.

Why? Because if you wanted it badly enough you would either already have achieved your goal, or be busy working on the way to achieving it. After researching thousands of people and their lives, I realized that if you have a burning desire to achieve a goal you will always achieve it, and figuring out how to do so isn't difficult. What is truly difficult for most people is to set goals that they would have a burning desire to achieve.

Desire is such a powerful engine that it will always get you from where you are to where you want to be. If you want your goal to be achieved, your desire to achieve it should be intense. And for the desire to be intense, your goal should include a big "What," big "Why" and big "Want."

Nothing great was ever achieved without enthusiasm. – Ralph Waldo Emerson

The starting point of all achievement is DESIRE. Keep this constantly in mind. Weak desire brings weak results, just as a small fire makes a small amount of heat. – Napoleon Hill

The only way to do great work is to love what you do. – Steve Jobs

Big What

As I am writing these words, in front of me is a book by Donald Trump with the title *Think Big and Kick Ass*. I like this title very much because it succinctly summarizes the secret of successful people, "Dream big and do the necessary work to achieve your goal." Successful people set big goals, not because they are so self-confident, not because they are greedy or insane, but because they know that big goals have much more energy behind them than small goals. If the goal is big for you, your desire to achieve it will also be big and as a result you will be much more likely to do the necessary work to achieve it.

At the age of 22, I set a goal to receive a Master of Business Administration degree. I realized, "The average candidate is 28 years old and has at least 5 years of experience in finance, supply chain management, marketing or strategy which I don't." In order to increase my chances, I decided to apply to 4 top 10 MBA programs in the U.S. where I had a burning desire to study, 2 second-tier schools in the U.S. and 1 school in the Ukraine. I thought, "Even if I fail to get accepted to a top MBA program I will definitely get accepted to one of the backup options."

In the winter, there was an event in Kyiv called "World MBA Tour" to which came admission officers and graduates from business schools from all over the world including top 10 MBA programs in the U.S. When I talked to representatives of these schools I felt goose bumps, I felt joy, and I felt excitement. On the way home it hit me, "Even a thought about one of the top 10 MBA programs in the U.S. makes me happy, even a thought about studying there gives me a huge amount of energy to do any work and overcome any obstacles. However, when I imagine myself studying at one of my backup options I feel no inspiration, no desire to do any work, no satisfaction. I realized that just getting an MBA degree wasn't a big enough goal for me to have a burning desire to achieve it, so I changed the goal slightly to "I want to receive a Master of Business Administration degree from one of the top 10 MBA programs in the U.S." Although this goal seemed impossible for me at the beginning, eventually I became the youngest person in the MBA program at the University of Michigan Ross School of Business.

Big dreams have big energy behind them. Big dreams motivate us to do things that we will never do for small dreams. Big dreams make our lives happier. When the goal isn't big enough, the desire to achieve it is low. When the goal isn't big enough, it's very easy to give up at the first sign of difficulties. When the goal isn't big enough, it's very difficult to persist no matter what.

Don't compromise your dreams, and settle for backup options, because in order to wake up every morning inspired, in order to have motivation to do necessary work and to overcome obstacles on the way to the goal, your goal needs to be BIG. Not BIG for your relatives, not BIG for your colleagues, not BIG for society but BIG for you. The goal should be big enough to stretch you, but not too huge to make it impossible to achieve.

My interest in life comes from setting myself huge, apparently unachievable challenges and trying to rise above them. – Sir Richard Branson

People are not lazy, they simply have impotent goals…that is…goals that do not inspire them. – Anthony Robbins

Dream big dreams; only big dreams have the power to move men's souls. – Marcus Aurelius, Roman emperor

Big Want

In our life we pursue many goals that other people say we should achieve. A manager says, "You should finish this report." Parents say, "You should clean your room," a teacher says, "You should do your homework," an advertisement says, "You should own an expensive car," society says, "You should have a secure job," and your friends say, "You should have your own house."

One of the biggest reasons people don't live the lives of their dreams is because they forget that the most important goals come not from external sources but from within. There is very little energy behind goals that other people set in front of us. When you work towards them, you experience laziness, you feel unmotivated, you don't persist and even once you achieve them it doesn't bring you satisfaction.

It's very easy to determine if the goal is your own by the words that you are using. If you say "I SHOULD have a nice car" then, most probably, you received this goal from external sources such as an advertisement, your friends or your spouse. If you say, "I WANT to have a nice car" then it's your own goal. Even though we don't notice it, when we refer to the goal that we truly want to achieve we use the word "Want" rather than "Should." If the goal is your OWN, then you will wake up excited to take necessary actions to achieve it but if the goal is not yours, you will be lazy. You can't get to the life of your dreams by achieving "Should" goals, but you can by achieving "Want" goals.

One of the secrets to happiness is to make sure that the majority of goals that you work towards are your OWN "I want" goals that are meaningful for you. Set goals that you want yourself, not the ones you pursue to please someone else or that others consider meaningful. The only way to get enough energy to do the necessary work, overcome obstacles and endure failures on the way to the goal is to have a burning desire to achieve it, and it's possible to have a burning desire to achieve a goal only if it's your OWN goal.

For example, when I decided to get an MBA degree at one of the top 10 universities in the U.S. it was my own goal. My mother thought that it was a bad idea, my friends said that taking a huge loan for education was insane, and none of my colleagues at work had an MBA degree from one of the top 10 schools in the U.S. or wanted one. This goal was my OWN goal and this is one of the main reasons why I managed to achieve it. If the goal matters deeply to you, there is no obstacle that could stop you on the way to achieving it. If the goal is your OWN, you will protect it, you will fight for it, you will battle for it, you will stand up for it and you will respect it.

Big Why

To make yourself truly desire to achieve a goal, you need to have a clear answer to the question, "Why is this goal important to me?" One of the biggest reasons why people don't achieve their goals is that their "Why" isn't big enough. A compelling reason why is what provides motivation to take actions towards what you want, to overcome obstacles and endure failures. Your "Why" should consist of the two biggest motivators of human beings: a pleasurable reward for achieving the goal and a painful consequence for not achieving it.

Firstly, imagine how your life will look like after you achieve your goal. List all the potential great things that you will experience once your desire is fulfilled. The more reasons you have and the more compelling they are, the bigger your desire will be to achieve a goal. The more desire you have, the more likely you are to get off the couch, do the necessary work and eventually achieve a goal. For example, if my goal is "I want to be able to do 50 pull-ups in 60 days," the potential benefits may be:

- I will look extremely fit and will be proud of my body.
- I will be able to record a video of myself doing 50 pull-ups and receive compliments from my friends.
- I will lose weight on the way to achieving my goal.
- In my childhood, I was never able to do more than 10 pull-ups on the bar, but always envied guys who could do tricks on the bar. Once I can do 50 pull-ups, I will be strong enough to learn tricks on the bar and fulfill my childhood dream.

Secondly, think about how your life will look like if your goal isn't achieved. List all the negative consequences if you don't fulfill your desire. Then amplify these negative consequences in your imagination, increase the feeling of pain and hate your future life without a fulfilled goal. For example, if your goal is "I want to lose 20 pounds by jogging on a treadmill and eliminating sweets from my diet within 3 months," a list of negative consequences of not reaching the goal may look like this:

- If I don't lose weight now, I might gain 30 more pounds within the next 3 years. I will look so ugly that my wife or husband will be ashamed to walk next to me.
- People with extra weight are more likely to get sick. I will suffer more diseases and will eventually die young.
- I won't have enough energy to do a great job in my business or in the company I work for. Eventually I won't self-realize or bring any value to the world and will be a failure.
- I will feel depressed and no amount of sweets will be able to make me any happier.

You can also make a consequence of not achieving a goal even more painful intentionally to increase your internal motivation to achieve it. For example, if your goal is to lose weight – wear clothes every day that you wore when you were much thinner. The discomfort from wearing clothes that are small will motivate you to lose weight quicker. Or make a commitment to people you respect that you will lose 20 pounds within 3 months. The pain from breaking your word and listening to their comments if you don't achieve a goal may motivate you even further.

Finally, make sure that both rewards and negative consequences are important and meaningful for you. The only goal of these pleasurable rewards and painful consequences is to evoke emotions in you, increase your desire to achieve a goal and motivate you to take action. Entice yourself with pleasurable rewards and scare yourself with negative consequences. If your "Why" is big enough for you, you will have such a burning desire to achieve a goal that you will do whatever it takes and no matter which obstacles you face on the way, you will achieve it sooner or later.

Emotional visualization test

A great way to check if you desire to achieve a particular goal badly enough is by using the emotional visualization test. Imagine as clearly as possible the moment when you have already achieved your goal. Clearly imagine what you see, hear and smell. Pay attention to how your body reacts. Do you feel happier? Do you feel excitement? Do you feel an internal smile? If yes, then you truly have a burning desire to achieve this goal and there are no walls that could stop you.

If you want to achieve a goal only in your head, chances are you don't have a burning desire to achieve it. You can deceive your head, but you can't deceive your body. If you don't have a burning desire to achieve a goal, your body will resist and scream, "Stop, this goal isn't yours. Don't take any actions to achieve it as you will waste time and effort but achievement of the goal won't bring you any joy."

This emotional test is a simple and effective way to test how important the goal is for you. In order to achieve a goal, you need to do a certain amount of work. And you will be motivated to do this work if your desire to achieve a goal is strong enough. Strong desire to achieve a goal evokes positive emotions even when you visualize a moment when it is achieved. A burning desire to achieve a goal will evoke emotions in you and these emotions are the fuel for your internal engine and drive your actions. If the goal evokes positive emotions, you will wake up excited. If the goal evokes positive emotions, you will feel goose bumps even by thinking about it. If the goal evokes positive emotions, you will feel an internal urge to take massive action to make your dream a reality.

In order for you to have a burning desire to achieve a goal, this goal should influence your emotions, as emotions are our main motivator. The goal that has a big What, a big Want and a big Why has a much bigger influence on emotions than a goal that doesn't and hence, has a much higher chance of being achieved. Listen to the voice of your body and test all your goals by the emotional visualization test. If a goal passes this test and you have strong enough desire to achieve it, you will not only definitely achieve the goal, but also the achievement of this goal will bring joy and happiness to your life.

When you are driving a car and want to get from one place to another, the two main things you need are clarity of what the destination is and enough fuel in the tank. If you want to achieve a goal, you also need to know exactly what it is and to have enough motivation inside. If you don't have enough desire to achieve a goal at the beginning of your trip, you will not only be unlikely to reach it but also will have no joy from reaching it.

You must have an intense, burning desire to achieve a goal in order to have enough internal fuel for the "vehicle" that will get you from where you are to where you want to be and you will have it if your goal has a big "What," a big "Why" and a big "Want."

Enjoy what you do as an exciting game

In the 1960s, Srully Blotnick, a PhD and psychologist, conducted a study of 1,500 people who wanted to become wealthy. He split them into two categories. Category A consisted of 1,245 people who said: "I am going to pursue money first and follow my passion later." Category B consisted of 255 people who said: "I am going to do what I am passionate about and trust that the money will follow later."

In 20 years, 101 people from the entire group became millionaires. What's interesting is that 100 millionaires were from Group B, where people specified following their passion as a first priority rather than money, and only 1 millionaire was from Group A. The group that consisted of only 17% studied accounted for 99% of the millionaires. Why is doing what you enjoy that important for achieving goals?

Everyone has the inner guidance system that tells you if you are working towards the right goal by the amount of joy you are experiencing in the process. Successful people always do what they love, because doing what you love is much more powerful fuel on the way to the goal than willpower. Work takes a significant amount of time in your life and if you enjoy what you do every day, you will not only achieve extraordinary results, but will also live a happy life.

If you enjoy what you do, you are much more likely to accomplish the amount of work necessary to achieve a goal, you wake up with anticipation to make progress and are very productive during the day, and you have a burning desire to act and perceive what you do as an exciting game, rather than a painful duty.

Make achieving goals a game

Psychologists have discovered that we are most productive when we are simultaneously relaxed, excited, open, confident, lively and playful. This state is called a high-performance state. What's interesting is that every time we are playing a game we are in a high-performance state. Hence, if you perceive the work you do as a game, you will do it with the highest performance.

Our attention is drawn to what is exciting and if you are doing a boring activity, you will be constantly distracted by things that are more interesting such as social media, computer games or chatting with friends. Find ways to make every task an entertaining game and you will not only enjoy your work more but also your productivity will grow significantly. For example, "I am checking how quickly I can finish these reports," "While running, I am listening to an interesting training on my Mp3 player" and "Let's see if I can accomplish more during the next hour than during the previous one."

Just like a car needs fuel to get from Point A to Point B, we need motivation to get from where we are to the desired goal. Enjoying what you do is one of the most powerful motivators in the world and can get you much further than willpower.

It is very hard to succeed in something unless you take the first step – which is to become very interested in it. – Warren Buffett

Success breeds success

Several years ago, while attending a conference in Las Vegas, I decided to have lunch in a cafeteria near a casino. At the door a lady asked, "Do you want to receive a 10% lunch discount? You can fill out this form to receive a free casino gambler's card that will allow you to both play at the casino and to receive a cafeteria discount." I said, "Sure, why not?" After I filled out the form, a casino representative took me to the 25¢ gambling machine and said, "Here is your card that is already preloaded with $3. After you play 12 times and use this $3 entirely, the card will be activated for use in the casino and cafeteria." I played 12 times, won $80 and the representative handed me the win in cash right away. I thought, "I went to the cafeteria to spend $15 on lunch but received not only a discount but also $80 in cash. What's the catch?"

During the conference I met David, who worked at a casino in the past, and he explained, "Andrii, the casino lets you win at the beginning to make you play longer and spend more money. Imagine that you came to the casino for the first time. You make a bet and lose. You make a second bet and lose. After you make a third bet and lose you say, 'Hey, it's impossible to win. It doesn't make sense to continue playing.' But what if you come to the casino for the first time and win several times in a row? Firstly, winning is pleasurable and you are motivated to experience this feeling again and again. Secondly, this success builds up your confidence that winning is possible. This self-confidence and motivation will allow you to persist in playing even after a long sequence of losses. You will think, 'Hey, I won in the past and it was pleasurable.

I can and I want to win again. The past losses are only temporary.'"

Achieving goals is similar to gambling and the more you succeed, the more you are motivated to succeed again and the more confident you are that succeeding is possible. After you achieve even a small goal, this small success will bring you to bigger success and bigger success will lead to a huge success and success grows like a snowball.

Every time you successfully reach a goal no matter how small, you make a contribution to your self-confidence and motivation piggy bank and tell yourself, "You see, I can succeed." The more success you experienced in the past, the higher is your confidence that you can overcome obstacles and sustain a long row of failures on the way to success. The more success you experienced in the past, the more pleasurable emotions you have experienced and the more motivation you have to experience even bigger success in the future because pleasurable emotions are addictive.

Just like in a casino, in order to do the necessary work to achieve a goal and win, you need to first experience small success in order to fill your self-confidence and motivation piggy bank and have a conviction: "I have succeeded in the past and also want and can succeed this time." Do you know why the probability of millionaires who went bankrupt to become millionaires again is many times higher than that of the average person? Because millionaires remember their past success, they have high confidence that becoming a millionaire is possible, and this confidence allows them to persist longer than a person who has never succeeded financially. Because millionaires remember their past success, unlike the average person they know that experiencing success is very pleasurable and the goal achievement is worth the effort. High achievers have bigger muscles for achieving goals than the majority of other people, because they train them by achieving goals of different sizes regularly.

Pursuing a big goal might be difficult at the beginning, but after you achieve a few initial successes, the rest of the way will be much easier. Experience success no matter how small, every day, to contribute to your piggy bank of self-confidence and motivation and create a huge internal power that will allow you to achieve any goal. For example, if you want to be able to do 100 pushups, increase the number of pushups you do during each training, if you want to learn a foreign language, memorize 10 new words during each class, or if you want to publish a novel, write 1 more page during each writing session. Aim to make small achievements regularly because success breeds success and the more success you experience, the more success you will draw in the future.

Success log and virtual support group

Your internal power that pushes you towards achievement is based on your self-confidence and motivation. Both self-confidence and motivation depend on memories of your past successes and moments when people who you respect believed in you. You can increase your internal power by using the following technique:

Firstly, remember a moment when you successfully achieved a goal that was highly important to you. So important that you were proud of yourself and felt like a rock star. In your imagination see what you saw at that time, hear what you heard at that time, and feel what you felt at that time. In a few minutes after you have recalled the moment that is associated with this achievement and experienced a feeling of success you felt at that time, your internal power will be increased. Next, repeat the same process with several more memories of your major achievements to increase the internal power even further. There is no moment when you are more motivated to take action and confident that you are capable of achieving any goal than after significant achievement. If you regularly recall past successes, your internal engine will become more powerful and will get you to the goals faster. A great thing to do is to write a list of your major achievements on a sheet of paper and to put it on the wall next to your desk so that when you occasionally look at it you remember what you have accomplished in the past and increase your internal power necessary to accomplish even more in the future.

Secondly, create your imaginary support group that will cheer you on while you take actions that bring you closer to the goal. Recall clearly the people who supported you the most in the past and their most encouraging words and compliments. For example, I remember when my math teacher said, "Andrii, I haven't ever seen anyone as purposeful as you. You are going to have a great future," I remember when my friend said, "Andrii, I believe that you will achieve anything you want," and I remember a guy who, after my presentation, said, "Andrii, it was the best speech I ever heard. I think you will become incredibly successful." All these people are your imaginary support group and they are ready to cheer you up again and again. Whenever you feel depressed or upset, remember people from your support group and the words they said and these memories will increase your self-confidence, motivation and internal power.

After you achieve a big goal or hear words of support from a person you respect, you experience a boost of self-confidence and motivation to make your dreams a reality. Every time you remember your major achievements or the words of the virtual support group, your subconscious believes that those moments are happening right now and as a result you become more self-confident and motivated to achieve your next goal. This technique not only gives extra fuel to your internal engine but also makes the process of goal achievement more enjoyable.

Support of other people in reaching your goal

In my childhood, I loved watching action movies about ninjas, samurais, kung fu and dreamed of learning karate. When my parents presented me with a manual written by Kiokushin Karate founder Masutatsu Oyama, I was on cloud nine and decided, "I will begin training right away!" I read the first 10 pages, tried several karate moves but in an hour got bored to death. I put away the manual and never practiced karate at home after that.

Later my parents enrolled me in the Kiokushin Karate school which I attended four times a week for several years. I not only learned fighting, participated in numerous competitions and received a blue belt, but also enjoyed every hour of training. Why was this approach much more successful than an attempt to learn karate through the book? The answer is –

communication with people. When people talk they exchange not only words but also their energy. Every time you interact with someone and this interaction is positive and relevant to your goal, your internal battery responsible for achieving this goal is charged. When I attended the karate school I listened to the trainer and my internal battery was charged, I interacted with single-minded students who had the same goal as I and my internal battery was charged, I discussed my classes with my parents and my internal battery was charged. My internal energy was high and as a result I had a huge desire to learn karate, trained as hard as I could and also enjoyed the process.

When you want to achieve a big goal, seek interaction with other people as much as possible to charge your internal battery with the necessary energy: find a mentor, talk with single-minded people who want to achieve a similar goal to yours, discuss your progress with friends or relatives, attend conferences, build a mastermind group or communicate on the internet. The more your internal battery is charged, the more motivation you have to achieve a goal, the more productively you act and the greater your success is. To achieve a big goal, you need a lot of energy, and positive communication with people is an excellent energy source that high achievers extensively use and a source of energy that you can't ignore.

Support from others is critical to your success. When you have support, the voices of encouragement soften the negative voices in your head. – Tammy Helfrich

There are two types of people – anchors and motors. You want to lose the anchors and get with the motors because the motors are going somewhere and they're having more fun. The anchors will just drag you down. — Wyland, world-renowned marine artist

Last 5 minutes of the day

Celebrate success and reward yourself

If you recognize all intermediate achievements during the day, you will become more motivated to take action because of the mental connection in your head: "Completing a task means pleasure." Every time you accomplish a step on the way to the goal, celebrate success to draw even more success in future. Celebrating means simply giving yourself pleasure as a reward for work well done.

Firstly, after completing a task, praise yourself, "I am super awesome! Great job!" "You are the man! Keep on going!" or "You are the best! I love you!" Praise is always pleasurable even if you praise yourself. If the task completed was really important, you can even do a winner's dance or brag to your colleague, friend or better half.

Secondly, to recognize completion of the task, you can strike a deal with yourself, "I will do this work now and then I will eat an apple," "I will work consistently for 30 minutes and then I will drink a coffee" or "I will meet this deadline successfully and then I will go for a short walk around the office."

Once I observed how animals are trained to do tricks in a circus. A trainer gives a command and every time an animal fulfills the command correctly, he rewards it with tasty food. After a while the animal fulfills a command correctly almost without failure because it knows, "Completing a command means pleasure." This method works extremely effectively not only for training animals but also for training our own subconscious mind. Reward yourself regularly for successfully completing steps on the way to the goal and you will be super productive in everything you do because of the reflex: "When I complete a task, it's pleasurable. I achieve a goal and I like it!" Celebrating every completed task within a day no matter how small will not only motivate you to work harder but will also make the process of goal achievement more pleasurable.

Daily progress and daily plan

In the evening just before going to bed briefly enter everything you have accomplished within a day into a dedicated computer file or notebook. Even if the task you completed wasn't big or you failed but learned a valuable lesson, write it down to keep track of your achievements. Next, go to the mirror, look yourself in the eyes and praise yourself for every accomplishment you made within a day, passionately and out loud.

Consider every day as a fierce competition against yesterday's you. Ask yourself in the evening: "Did I get at least one step closer to my goal today compared to yesterday?" If the answer is yes, you win this competition and if you win this competition regularly you will achieve any goal sooner than you think. Aim to accomplish the maximum within a day and finish each day successfully because you get closer to your long-term goal by achieving your short-term daily goals.

If you know, "At the end of each day I'll record the results and celebrate the accomplishments," you will be motivated to do as much as possible within a day and as a result will reach a goal sooner. This technique of writing down and celebrating the accomplishments in the evening will help to track what you have done and increase motivation to take action.

In the evening just before going to bed in addition to writing down the results of the day also write down a list of tasks you want to complete tomorrow. If you clearly understand what to do in the morning, you will act without procrastination and focus on tasks that have the biggest impact on how soon you achieve a goal. According to the Dominican University study, people who create a plan and regularly check their results increase their chances of achieving a goal by at least 15%.

You might ask, "Does it matter if I write a plan for the day in the evening of the day before or in the morning?" If you write a list of action items in the evening, your subconscious mind will think the entire night about how to fulfill tasks from the list most effectively. When you sleep your subconscious mind processes thousands of thought combinations and by the time you wake up will generate ideas valuable for accomplishing the tasks. Planning your next day before going to bed is a very effective strategy to increase productivity and subsequent success.

Imagine that you could accomplish only one task tomorrow. Which task would it be so that after the evening review session you would still consider the day more or less successful? Identify the most important task from the list by answering this question, then in the morning concentrate on this task single-mindedly until it's 100% complete. Accomplishment of the most important task will charge your enthusiasm to successfully complete the rest of the tasks from the list and will set the tone for the rest of the day. Creating a plan for the day makes your actions focused; however, if you also specify the most important task from the list that you will accomplish first, you will make your actions laser focused and your time will be spent as effectively as possible.

Before going to bed, spend 5 minutes on summarizing what you have accomplished during the day, celebrating your success and writing down a plan for tomorrow. Although this ritual takes very little time it is one of the most powerful techniques that high achievers use and can increase your productivity and satisfaction from the process of goal achievement multiple times.

Follow effective action with quiet reflection. From the quiet reflection will come even more effective action. – Peter Drucker

The Idea Lifestyle

In order to make your life happier, you need to generate ideas of what exactly you want. Once you have created an idea of what exactly you want, then you need to generate plenty of ideas daily of how to accomplish each particular task on the way to achievement of your goal. After the goal is achieved, you again need to generate ideas of what else you want to achieve and this cycle goes in circles and never ends. As you can see, fulfillment of dreams highly depends on how effectively you can generate ideas and in this section we will discuss three principles that most creative people in the world use and that will help you to generate as many brilliant ideas as you need in the shortest time possible.

Think and Rest

Numerous research studies were conducted to compare the performance of our right brain (subconscious mind) and left brain (conscious mind). The results confirmed that our creative right brain is at least 2 million times faster than our analytical left brain. The analytical left brain is responsible for judging, self-monitoring and internal dialogue. It prevents you from saying everything you think and doing everything you consider. The right brain is responsible for generating new creative ideas. The right brain is responsible for all activities that involve creativity and can process enormous amounts of information within seconds.

Many people think, "In order to generate ideas, I simply need to sit for few hours and think about a problem until I generate one great idea." In fact, this approach rarely gives good results because it contradicts with principles of subconscious thinking. The most effective thinking technique that world-class thinkers use daily is Think and Rest because it allows the subconscious mind to produce successful ideas quickly and with little effort.

Firstly, for 30 minutes, 60 minutes or several hours, think about the problem and how to solve it and write down all ideas that come to your mind, no matter how crazy they are. Aim to generate as many ideas as possible because in the world of creativity quantity equals quality and the more ideas you generate, the higher chances are that one of them will be brilliant. During this initial thinking stage you not only generate ideas but also let your subconscious mind know which ideas you need. If your problem is simple, you may find a good solution already during this initial brainstorming session, but if you don't find an appropriate solution within the first several hours, forget about your problem completely and get back to your everyday life.

Secondly, after you stop thinking about the problem consciously, your subconscious will continue thinking about it 24/7. When you think about the problem you give your subconscious mind a command, "I am interested in finding a solution for this problem. Please generate ideas for me." After the subconscious mind receives a command during the time when you don't consciously focus on the problem, it makes random connections between millions of thoughts in the back of your mind and once it sees that one of the connections seems interesting says, "Hey, here is one more good idea for you." The subconscious mind generates most of your best ideas after you have forgotten about the problem and during moments you least expect them. Whether an idea pops into your head while you are in the shower, waiting in line or falling asleep – write it down instantly.

Finally, think about your problem occasionally for 2 to 5 minutes. During this time, you will not only generate fresh ideas but will also reactivate your creative mind and make it think intensively while you are not consciously thinking about the problem. The difference between days when you generate plenty of excellent ideas and days when you generate zero ideas is simply whether you gave your subconscious mind a task or not. Thinking about a problem for a few minutes several times during the day will make your subconscious mind work intensively on the problem 24/7 and generate excellent ideas in abundance. The subconscious mind is especially productive while you sleep because it isn't blocked by the analytical brain, that's why it will be very rewarding if one of the times you think about the problem is before you go to bed. Just 10 to 15 minutes of thinking a day about your tasks is more than enough to activate your subconscious mind to work on ideas and to turn your dreams into reality.

The Think and Rest technique doesn't take much time; however, it activates the subconscious mind and makes it think about the problem day and night and as a result generates valuable ideas as productively as possible. The Think and Rest technique helps the best innovators and thinkers to generate successful ideas in 100% of cases. If after using this technique a great idea still doesn't come to you, it means that either not enough time has passed or your subconscious mind doesn't have enough raw materials to create ideas from. You might ask, "What are raw materials for creativity?" About that in the next section…

I have found, for example, that if I have to write upon some rather difficult topic, the best plan is to think about it with very great intensity – the greatest intensity of which I am capable – for a few hours or days, and at the end of that time give orders, so to speak (to my subconscious mind) that the work is to proceed underground. After some months I return consciously to the topic and find that the work has been done. – Bertrand Russell, the British logician and mathematician

Expose yourself to new experiences

One day little Jimmy went to his best friend Suzy's house and noticed the beautiful constructions she built from a Lego set. He looked at cars, ships and castles and decided, "I want to build beautiful Lego constructions, too."

Jimmy took two little pieces of a Lego set that he owned. He spent hours looking at them and trying to put them together in all possible combinations but realized that no matter what he did these 2 pieces never looked like a car, a ship or a castle. He went to Suzy and said, "Suzy, I am just not creative enough to build beautiful Lego constructions." Suzy looked at him, smiled and said, "Jimmy, you have the talent to create beautiful Lego constructions. You just don't have enough constructor pieces. I have been collecting my Lego pieces for years and now have thousands of them. If you had as many pieces as I do, you would easily create even better constructions."

Ideas are combinations of other ideas and the more diverse life experiences you have, the more different ideas you will be able to construct. Many people say, "I can't create great business ideas. I am not creative." However, the true reason why they fail is that they have too few different experiences in their memory to construct new ideas from.

The world's greatest thinkers have an insatiable curiosity and actively seek new experiences that can increase the amount of their creative constructor pieces. They travel, make new acquaintances, try various hobbies, attend conferences and seminars, and read books, magazines and blogs. In the world of creativity, the wealthy person is not the one who has more money but the one who has more experiences to build ideas from.

People whose life follows the same pattern for years may find themselves in a situation like little Jimmy who tried to create something incredible from just several pieces of a Lego set. Constantly bombard your brain with new ideas and experiences which will become raw materials for your future successful ideas. The more different experiences you have had in life, the more ideas of others you have learned, the more creative combinations your brain will be able to make and the more valuable ideas it will generate. If you want to be a world-class thinker, a quest for new creative raw materials should become your habit.

Creativity is just connecting things. When you ask creative people how they did something, they feel a little guilty because they didn't really do it, they just saw something. It seemed obvious to them after a while. That's because they were able to connect experiences they've had and synthesize new things. And the reason they were able to do that was that they've had more experiences or they have thought more about their experiences than other people. Unfortunately, that's too rare a commodity. A lot of people in our industry haven't had very diverse experiences. So they don't have enough dots to connect, and they end up with very linear solutions without a broad perspective on the problem. – Steve Jobs

I really had a lot of dreams when I was a kid, and I think a great deal of that grew out of the fact that I had a chance to read a lot. – Bill Gates

Train creative muscles

When I was in 7th grade, my math teacher Alexander said to my mother, "Victoria, your son's performance is very poor. Honestly, I think math isn't his thing. It would be better for Andrii if you transfer him to another school at the end of the year." My classmate Peter was a naturally gifted student and several heads above everyone I knew at math. He always solved problems nobody else could and Alexander called him "math heavy artillery."

In 8th grade, after one incident in class I became very interested in math. I began devoting all my spare time to math and by the end of the year became the second-best math student in the class after Peter. In 9th grade, Peter became very interested in guitar, founded his own band and neglected math. By the end of the 9th grade, I outperformed Peter and became the strongest math student in the entire school. In 10th grade, I continued devoting at least 4 hours a day to solving problems and by the end of the year became one of the 100 best math students in the Ukraine.

Peter is certainly much more gifted than I am, but I trained significantly more. I am sure that if he devoted at least half the time that I did to math he would achieve far better results than I. If you are interested to know what happened to Peter later, he became a guitar player in one of the most popular bands in the Ukraine.

When people see a person who can do 100 pushups they don't say, "Wow this person was born with a gift to do pushups. Unfortunately, I don't have a talent for pushups and will never be able to do as many pushups as he (or she)." Everybody knows that if you want to be able to do 100 pushups you simply need to develop your chest muscles by doing pushups regularly for several months. It's a common belief that people who can generate excellent ideas quickly have a special talent, however in reality these people just have bigger creative muscles because they think about ideas more often than others. If you practice generating ideas regularly, after some time your creative muscles will become stronger, your subconscious will process random combinations of thoughts faster and you will produce better ideas than the majority of naturally gifted people.

Many people rarely give tasks to their subconscious mind and as a result when they realize that their creative muscles are weak say, "I just don't have talent for creating ideas." This sounds the same as, "I exercise only twice a year and can't do more than 5 pushups. I don't have the talent for pushups."

The more you practice pushups, the more pushups you will be able to do. The same happens with ideas. The more you practice creative thinking, the quicker high-quality ideas will come to your mind. If you take practicing idea generation seriously, in a few years your creative muscles will be so strong that other people may call you a creative genius.

The Idea Lifestyle Bundle

Certainly, every child is born blessed with a vivid imagination. But just as muscles grow flabby with disuse, so the bright imagination of a child pales in later years if he ceases to exercise it. – Walt Disney

If you want to make your life an exciting adventure, ideas should become your lifestyle. If you have an "idea lifestyle," you first generate ideas about what you want, then you generate ideas about how to achieve what you want and finally you take actions and achieve it. The life experiences you gained on the way to achievement of the goal will serve as valuable raw material for creating new desirable goals and for even greater quality ideas of how to achieve these new goals. And this sequence will go in circles over and over again. The more ideas you generate, the more goals you set and achieve, the more experiences you have, the bigger creative muscles you build and these lead to even more ideas.

The quantity and quality of ideas that you create are essential for goal achievement and once you make ideas your lifestyle, they will come to you much more often because your creative muscles will be stronger and your creative constructor will have more pieces. Once you make the idea lifestyle your lifestyle, become obsessed about ideas and make them one of your core values, you will succeed in all areas of life, fulfill all your dreams and make your life an exciting adventure.

All achievements, all earned riches, have their beginning in an idea. – Napoleon Hill, American self-help guru

Final Checklist

Before we get to the end of the book I want you to give yourself a present. Complete a "100 dreams" exercise and choose one dream from the list, fulfillment of which will bring you the biggest joy. Make a commitment to fulfill this dream and take the first step towards living a life of your dreams right now. All of the information in *The Achievement Factory* may help you to achieve goals more effectively, however let me remind you of the five core foundations that you might use for achievement of the dream you have chosen most often.

1. **Set a specific and measurable goal**

This step might take you just a few minutes, however it might have the biggest impact on whether you achieve your dream or not. Formulate your dream as a specific and measurable goal to set a direction for your actions clearly. The more specific and measurable a goal is, the more precise and impactful will be your actions and the sooner your dream will become a reality.

2. **Visualize a goal**

Visualization is one of the most powerful techniques that high achievers use to fulfill their dreams because it is incredibly effective. Visualization allows you to increase your desire to achieve a goal, to activate the subconscious to generate valuable ideas, to increase focus and to set an internal filter to notice relevant resources. The visualization magic formula says clarity of visualization X regularity of visualization = achieved goal.

3. Last 5 minutes of the day

At the end of each day check the progress you have made during the day and celebrate success. Also, set a plan of what you want to accomplish tomorrow. This short ritual will make you more motivated to take actions, will make each of your days more productive and will make the path towards achievement of the goal shorter.

4. Think and Rest

The subconscious mind (the creative brain) is responsible for generating ideas and ideas are essential for achievement of any goal. The subconscious mind stays idle if you don't activate it by giving it problems to solve. Use the Think and Rest technique daily to keep the subconscious mind thinking about how to achieve a goal most effectively and you will get excellent ideas in abundance. Every time a great idea comes to your mind, evaluate it and if it can help you to achieve a goal add it to your action plan.

5. Take massive action

Of course in order to achieve a goal you need to take massive action. In terms of actions two things are important to remember. Focus your attention as much as possible on the goal, because the longer you focus on the goal within a day, the more actions you take. Secondly, remember that according to the Law of Inertia it's very difficult to begin taking actions, but once you have overcome the initial resistance you will be taking massive action daily with pleasure and without much effort.

After fulfilling this dream, give yourself presents regularly and your life will always be happy and full of exciting adventures. Remember that you can achieve anything you want if you have a desire and make a commitment. Repeat after me, "My life is in my hands. I promise to live happily and fulfill all my dreams no matter how big they are." Now you have your own Achievement Factory that, if managed properly, will make your life an exciting adventure.

The poorest man in the world is the man without a dream. The most frustrated man in the world is the man with a dream that never becomes reality. – Myles Munroe

The Idea Lifestyle Bundle

The Idea Lifestyle Bundle

The Business Idea Factory

A World-Class System for Creating Successful Business Ideas

Andrii Sedniev

The Idea Lifestyle Bundle

Introduction

Imagine that you were born in the 16th century. Your occupation and future would be mostly predetermined by the family you were born into. If you wanted to become successful, you would have to be born into the family of a king, a bishop or a wealthy trader. Luckily those days are gone.

We live in the idea age. Companies succeed because of great ideas and go bankrupt because of lack of them. Some of the most successful companies such as Microsoft, Walmart, Apple and Honda became successful not because of the wealth and social status of the families their founders were born into, but because of the ideas behind them.

Imagine what your life might look like if you could improve the quantity and quality of business ideas that you generate, multiple times. You could create a business that would change the world. You could change the lives of millions of people and leave a mark in history. You could make each of your days more adventurous and interesting.

In 1968 George Land and Beth Jarman gave a test, used by NASA to measure the creativity of engineers and scientists, to 1,600 five-year-old kids. Later, they gave the same test to kids at the age of 10 and 15. The results showed that at the age of five, 98% of children demonstrate genius level of creativity; at the age of 10, about 30% of children demonstrate genius level of creativity, and at the age of 15, only 10%. The same test was given to a group of adults and among them only 2% showed genius level of creativity.

Children are extremely creative but when they begin going to school their creativity drops significantly. In school, children learn that there is only one answer for each question and are requested to conform to conventional social wisdoms The difference between geniuses and most of us is that they managed to not lose their childhood creativity.

The great news is that you can significantly improve your ability to generate successful business ideas. Over the last 10 years I have researched business idea generation techniques used by the world's best scientists, entrepreneurs, CEOs and innovators. I carefully collected and analyzed every small bit of wisdom that may increase the number and quality of business ideas that one can produce. As a result, the *Business Idea Factory* system was created which describes an extremely effective and easy-to-use process for creating successful business ideas.

I promise that if you apply the strategies described in this book daily, you will increase the number and quality of business ideas that you create multiple times. After my students and I began using this system, the number and quality of business ideas that we produced increased hundreds of times. Many people began new businesses after reading this book, significantly increased revenue in their existing businesses and became more successful. I promise that if you take the techniques described in this book seriously and begin implementing them today, your life will change for the better. There are few things that can bring as much joy and success in business as the moment when an excellent idea comes into your head. Are you ready to build your business idea factory? Let's begin.

Creative brain vs. analytical brain

Activate your super-fast brain

Numerous research studies were conducted to compare the performance of our right brain (subconscious mind) and left brain (conscious mind). The results confirmed that our creative right brain is at least 2 million times faster than our analytical left brain. The analytical left brain is responsible for judging, self-monitoring and internal dialogue. It prevents you from saying everything you think and doing everything you consider. The right brain is responsible for generating new creative ideas.

In his research at Johns Hopkins University, Charles Limb asked jazz musicians and rap artists to compose an improvisational piece of music. While they were playing, Charles measured the activity of different areas of the brain. During this creative improvisation, the part of the brain responsible for analytical thinking and judgment showed much lower activity.

The right brain is responsible for all activities that involve creativity and can process enormous amounts of information within seconds. The conscious mind is not only useless for generating business ideas but, in fact, blocks the subconscious mind from doing its work. To become world class at generating business ideas you need to learn how to turn your analytical brain off and let the subconscious mind think.

If you want to effectively generate business ideas, you need to avoid any activities that engage the left brain that blocks the subconscious mind. When you think about your task, remember 3 rules: no judging, no criticizing and no internal dialoguing.

Walt Disney strategy

Walt Disney was certainly one of the most creative people in the 20th century. With his skill of generating successful business ideas, he built one of the biggest media conglomerates in the world. Walt Disney created fantastical ideas that might have sounded crazy and unfeasible at first glance, then considered how to make these fantasies a reality and finally evaluated them. In the process of generating new ideas, Walt separated his thinking into 3 stages: Dreamer, Realist and Critic.

A Dreamer generates creative ideas. There are no limitations and your imagination can take you anywhere. Imagine that you have a magic wand and everything is possible. For the Dreamer, cats can fly, houses are made of ice cream, TVs have legs and dance. At this stage your goal is to create and write down as many ideas as possible and the crazier they are, the better. You will have multiple opportunities to judge your ideas later, but while being a Dreamer turn off your analytical left brain. Judging and evaluating block your creative subconscious mind.

The Realist answers the question, "How can I make this idea a reality?" At this stage, you decide how to adopt or modify the idea to make it practical for the market. Even if you decide to discard the idea later, you need to first ponder how to make it real and how it can be combined with your other ideas. Give each idea a chance to live before criticizing it.

As the Critic, you should identify potential flaws of the idea. Why might it not work? What potential problems and difficulties in implementation could your idea have? Most important for you is to begin judging and evaluating ideas only after you have been a Dreamer and Realist. The majority of people criticize their ideas at the Dreamer stage and not only block the idea generation process, but kill the ideas too early. Often the idea may sound crazy at the beginning, but with slight modification or in combination with other ideas may lead to a successful business.

In 1943 Edwin Land took a picture of his 3-year-old daughter. She asked, "Dad, why can't I see the picture that you have taken right away?" Edwin thought about how to make this idea a reality and in 4 years the first Polaroid camera was released. Had the daughter of Edwin Land known why pictures couldn't be made instantaneously or had Edwin discarded her idea instantly instead of first thinking about how to make it a reality, the world would never have seen Polaroid.

Whenever you think about ideas always separate dreaming and judging. These two processes don't get along well. This simple thinking strategy can have a dramatic impact on the quantity and quality of ideas that you generate.

I just need one big idea

If you asked me: "Andrii, can you say what events have influenced your life the most?" a conversation with James in

New York's JFK Airport would be certainly one of the events I mention.

James was sitting next to me at the departure gate waiting for his flight to Charlotte and began a casual conversation. I learned that James had successfully sold several IT companies for more than $100M. However, what impressed me even more was that with all this money he was traveling in economy class and was dressed in a way that would never reveal that he is rich.

In the middle of the conversation I said, "You know, James, I truly envy your entrepreneurial gift. Since childhood I have dreamt about starting a company like Microsoft, but realized that I have no talent of generating great business ideas."

James smiled at me and said, "Really? How did you come to this conclusion?"

"Since childhood I wanted to become an entrepreneur but couldn't stumble upon a big business idea that could make me rich and famous like Bill Gates. A year ago I decided, 'I will lock myself in a room and will think until I come up with a big business idea or until I give up on becoming an entrepreneur.' For eighteen hours straight I was thinking and staring at the wall, thinking and staring at the ceiling, thinking and walking back and forth. I didn't come up with an outstanding business idea and gave up on my childhood dream."

"Andrii, you might not know this, but before Microsoft, Bill Gates created Traf-O-Data, a company that prepared reports for traffic engineers based on data from roadway traffic counters. This company didn't have big success but the experience was very valuable for creating Microsoft.

"When I became an entrepreneur with my first company I lost money, and my second company brought me less income per year than if I worked for minimum wage. But without the first 2 companies I would never have enough experience and knowledge to create the third company that I eventually sold for over $40M.

"Andrii, forget about a big idea. Your chances of creating it while staring at the wall are less than winning the lottery. Just begin implementing any of your business ideas and in the process many bigger ideas will come to you. Great ideas are created based on your life experiences and to get them you should be actively doing something."

This short conversation with James changed my attitude towards entrepreneurship. Had I not met James, I might still not have opened my own business and have joy from seeing how my students generate excellent business ideas daily and become successful.

When I talk to people I often hear, "Andrii, I envy your entrepreneurial gift. I'd like to start my own business but I don't have enough starting capital and a big business idea." I always say, "Just begin implementing today the best business ideas that you have with the starting capital that you have. In the process you will learn how to promote, how to sell, how to collaborate with other people, how to generate ideas and solve problems. Once you hit a really big business idea, you will have enough experience and resources to make it a success."

Exercise: A $100 hour

A $100 hour is one of my favorite exercises for generating business ideas. It will help you create many interesting ideas, some of which may bring enormous success.

Think for one hour about how you can make an extra $100. In this exercise you don't need to think about how to change the world, how to become a billionaire or how to create a steady stream of income. Your only goal is to generate as many ideas as possible of how you can earn an extra $100. That's it. After the completion of the exercise, pick the one idea that you like the most and make a commitment to implement it. After you implement this business idea you will know if it works, if you can scale it and if you can outsource some tasks.

The $100 hour technique is very easy and fun to do and it can bring your business enormous success. Your subconscious mind may be paralyzed by the thought, "I have to create a big business idea that will change my life," but it will eagerly generate business ideas that can bring an extra $100. Some of these ideas will become big, profitable and successful businesses. The $100 hour technique will bring you many interesting ideas, but only under the condition that you do it regularly. When you are ironing, jogging, gardening, waiting in line or feeling bored during a corporate meeting, it's a wonderful time for the $100 hour.

Programming the mind

During the day

One day I went to the stadium near my house to jog and after several rounds a question popped up in my head: "Why are there days when I create hundreds of excellent ideas and there are other days when I create zero ideas?" In a few minutes I realized why this happens, and thought, "Thank you, universe, for sending me this insight. I see how it can make a huge impact on my ability to generate successful business ideas. This is perhaps the biggest gift I ever received."

Once you learn the difference between generating hundreds of excellent ideas per day and no ideas at all you may think, "Hey, Andrii, it's logical and obvious." However, this simple insight can increase the number and quality of ideas you produce many times. In fact, if you take this insight seriously people will think that you are a genius.

The day when you create hundreds of ideas, you ask yourself questions and give your brain problems to think about: "How do I draw more visitors to my company website? What other products can my company produce? How do I increase sales?" The day you create zero ideas, is the day you don't give your brain any tasks. If you don't know what ideas you need, your brain simply remains idle and your subconscious mind doesn't do any work.

In the 1960s my grandmother saw a computer for the first time in her life. Her brother, Yuriy, brought her to the computer lab of the university where he worked and said, "Alina, this is one of the most powerful computers of our time. There are less than 10 such computers in the Ukraine." My grandma asked, "It's almost 1 a.m. Why are there people still working here?"

"You see, Alina, there is only one computer in the entire university and it's extremely expensive and powerful. Professors and PhD students are sharing time on it and it's never idle."

If you want to become a world-class business ideas creator, your brain should also never be idle. No, I don't mean that you need to work hard or be thinking for hours about your problems. You just need to decide which ideas you need and give your brain tasks. If you just think about several problems for, say, 15 minutes a day, it will be enough to set a program for your subconscious mind. It will process millions of combinations while you exercise at the gym, have lunch with your friend or while you sleep. Eventually you will get many new ideas in the form of insight or a creativity spark.

Realizing which ideas you need and giving your brain tasks daily is the difference between creating thousands of ideas and no ideas at all. It is also the difference between enormous success in business and no success at all.

Before you sleep

Several years ago I was an audience member during a corporate presentation. I remember a speaker saying, "If you want to work at my company, you may expect to work about 16 hours per day." Somebody in the audience asked, "Does this time include sleep?" And the audience burst out in laughter.

In fact, sleep time can be the most productive time for generating business ideas if you know how to use it properly. While you sleep the subconscious mind works even more productively than during the day because it's not blocked by the analytical brain. However, it will generate outstanding business ideas for you only if you activate it properly.

You may ask, "Andrii, how can I activate my subconscious mind before I go to bed?" While I was a high school student I often worked on solving math problems until late. When I got stuck on a particular problem and got tired, I went to bed. Very often, when I woke up in the morning, I had an idea of how to proceed with solving the problem.

When you think about your task just before sleep, it's the same as telling your subconscious, "Here is a question I need an answer for. Please generate ideas for me." Your subconscious gets the message and works the entire night while you sleep. Once you think about the task again in the morning you will get valuable ideas. The subconscious doesn't speak our language, but conveys ideas through intuition or gut feeling. Don't try to understand where the ideas come from. It's impossible. Just expect them to come.

Trust your subconscious mind and appreciate what it does for you.

Glass of water technique

"Glass of water" is one of the most effective and powerful creativity techniques that exist. It's extremely easy to use, however it can make miracles with your ability to generate excellent ideas while you sleep. The author of this technique is Jose Silva, who became famous worldwide by developing a complex of psychological exercises called the Silva Method.

Take a water glass and fill it with clean but not boiled water. With both hands, take the glass, close your eyes and look upward at a 45-degree angle. Formulate a task that you need to solve as a question. Then, drink half of the glass of water while thinking, "This is all I need to find the solution to the problem I have in mind."

Open your eyes. Put the glass of water near the bed and go to sleep without talking to anyone. In most cases you will receive an answer while you sleep in the form of a hint, insight or partial idea. Once you wake up, immediately write down all ideas, memories and thoughts that come to mind. Drink the second half-glass of water and thank your subconscious for the work that was done.

If you didn't get a satisfying answer, close your eyes, look slightly upward and drink the second half-glass of water while thinking, "This is all I need to find the solution to the problem I have in mind." The idea for the problem's solution will come to you during the day. And one more thing, believe that ideas will come to you.

You might think, "Can I use a cup instead of the glass? Can I say a different phrase while drinking the water? Can I do this technique without water at all?" This technique works most effectively if you don't change anything. It's critical to use a glass, it's critical what you say, and it's critical that you expect ideas to come. Follow these instructions as a ritual. It works in 100% of the cases for me, it works for thousands of people who tried it, and it will work for you.

Genius inventors realize that many breakthrough ideas came to them while they slept. If you need a creative business idea, don't sit at your desk until late. The subconscious processes millions of thoughts while you are not consciously thinking about the problem and sleep is a time when it works best. Just go to bed, let your subconscious know what problem needs to be solved and in the morning write down all thoughts that come to your head.

Set a task

Ask the right question

Before generating business ideas you need to decide which problem or task you will think about. Asking the right question is extremely critical because it will determine the direction in which your brain will think and the type of ideas your subconscious will generate. For example, if you lived in the 19th century and asked: "How can I create faster horses?" you might have gotten ideas about how to create a breed of faster horses or develop an effective training for horses. However, if you asked, "How can I get people from point A to point B faster?" you might have invented a car, a train or a plane.

Several questions are better than one

You may ask, "Andrii, it's easy to know which question to ask looking into the past. How can I know which question is right for my problem that hasn't been solved yet?" Well, the more questions you ask, the higher the chance of finding a right question and generating a successful idea.

Spend 10 minutes thinking about your problem. Quickly write down at least 10 different versions of the question you want to answer. Do not judge or evaluate questions so as to not activate the analytical left brain. Your goal is to create as many questions as possible no matter how crazy or unreasonable. Pick several questions that will allow you to look at the problem from different perspectives. If while working on the problem you think in several different directions, your chances of finding a successful business idea will be higher.

For example, if you want to answer the question, "How can I increase sales of the washing machines that my plant produces?" you may express the same concept in the following ways: "How can I sell more than one washing machine to each customer?" "What new products can I sell?" "How can the plant increase the revenue?" "How can I sell washing machines not just to households, but also to companies?" "How can I effectively promote the washing machines?" "How can I increase the quality of my washing machines?" "How can I hire or train the most qualified sales representatives in the market?" Thinking about each of these questions may bring you to the solution that the first question won't.

Sometimes you don't create the successful business idea simply because you asked the wrong question. No matter how experienced or talented you are, you won't arrive at the right question every single time. If while thinking on your problem you change questions occasionally, it will increase the quality and quantity of successful ideas that you create. Always remember that the direction in which you think may predetermine your ideas.

Questions that bring results

Your questions should be specific and action oriented for your subconscious to generate excellent ideas. For example, instead of "Why don't I have money to buy a new car?" ask

"How can I earn enough money to buy a new Honda Civic?" After asking a first question, your subconscious mind may answer without thinking, "Because you don't earn enough to buy a car." If you ask a second question in the example, your subconscious will suggest specific strategies for earning more money. It will also know how much money you need exactly and suggest the ideas accordingly.

After becoming CEO of Ford, Donald Petersen replaced sophisticated rules that a design center had to follow for creating new cars with a simple guideline: "Design something that you would be proud to park in your driveway." This change in direction for the brains of Ford engineers allowed them to design the highly successful Ford Taurus.

Toyota management asked employees, "Please give ideas of how the company can become more productive" and received very few ideas. Later they reworded the question to "How can you make your job easier?" and received an enormous amount of valuable ideas.

Edward Jenner invented the smallpox vaccine by changing a question from "How can we prevent smallpox?" to "Why don't milkmaids get smallpox?"

In many instances, if you can't create a successful business idea, it means that you simply asked a wrong question. When you are stuck and don't make any progress, spend some time restating a question. By describing a problem in several different ways, you will look at it from different perspectives and generate different ideas. Even a tiny change in the question that you ask yourself may dramatically improve the quantity and quality of business ideas that your subconscious will generate.

Pyramid of problems

Change abstraction level of the question

Each question you ask has an abstraction level. By decreasing or increasing the abstraction level, you may stimulate your brain to come up with new ideas you haven't ever thought about. An excellent technique for changing an abstraction level of the problem is the "5 Whys" technique. For example, if you want to create ideas that will answer the question, "How can I increase sales of the T54 model of washing machines that my plant produces?" ask "Why" 5 times.

Step 1: Why do you want to sell more T54 washing machines? "Because I want to sell more washing machines overall."

Step 2: Why do you want to sell more washing machines? "Because I want to improve overall sales."

Step 3: Why do you want to improve overall sales? "To make my business more profitable."

Step 4: Why do you want to make your business more profitable? "To increase my personal wealth."

Step 5: Why do you want to increase your personal wealth? "To earn enough money, so that I can work less and spend more time with my family."

Answering each of the following questions will allow you to generate ideas that will solve your problem: "How can I work less and spend more time with my family?" "How can I increase my personal wealth?" "How can I make my business more profitable?" "How can I increase overall sales?" "How can I sell more washing machines?" and "How can I sell more T54s?" Once you change an abstraction level to a higher or a lower one, you may come up with ideas that you weren't able to create with a previous question. For example, if you phrase a question as "How can I increase overall sales?" you may come up with an idea to begin producing laundry dryers in addition to washing machines. And if you phrase the question as "How can I work less and spend more time with my family?" you can come up with an idea to delegate some tasks to an assistant or to optimize your work processes.

Changing the abstraction level of your question will change the direction of your thinking. Sometimes you might think, "Oh, it's a dead end. I just can't come up with a really good idea." However, the real problem is not that you don't get appropriate ideas, but that you directed your thinking to the wrong path. Change an abstraction level of the problem or reword a question and completely different ideas will come to your head. Be sure that one of them will be a perfect solution for your task.

Break a problem into pieces

Many years ago I asked a serial entrepreneur, multimillionaire and exceptional problem-solver, "Jason, imagine that you want to launch a new business. How would you decide which actions to take first?"

"Andrii, if I wake up in the morning and decide to become a chocolate producer, I break this complex task into several simpler ones: 'How can I produce tasty chocolates?' and 'How can I sell many chocolates?'

"Each of these problems I split into several even smaller problems. 'How can I produce tasty chocolates?' may be split into: 'How do I get a recipe for tasty chocolate?' and 'How do I outsource production of my chocolate?' The task, 'How can I sell many chocolates?' may be split into: 'How can I sell chocolates through supermarkets?' and 'How can I promote chocolates through media?'

"All tasks get split into smaller tasks until they get so small that by thinking about them, I can come to specific actions that need to be taken.

"I use this strategy every day for solving complex business tasks. Andrii, if you want to solve a complex problem, just build a pyramid from smaller problems and you will be able to solve tasks that seem unsolvable from the first glance."

Once you create an idea of what business you want to be in, the process of generating business ideas only begins. You will need to create thousands of smaller ideas that will answer questions about how to implement each element of the business such as: promotion, hiring talent, outsourcing product development, marketing or sales. Practice changing the abstraction level of your questions and you will be easily able to switch between strategic tasks and everyday implementation tasks. Practice splitting big tasks into smaller ones and there will be no problem for which you can't create a brilliant solution. Remember that businesses become great one idea at a time.

Imagine that you work for minimum wage and you have a childhood dream to travel around the world for 6 months on a luxurious yacht. You ask yourself, "How can I earn $200,000 to buy a luxurious yacht for my trip?" After brainstorming for a week, you come to a conclusion, "With my current salary there is no way I can make my childhood dream a reality." Let's see how applying techniques from this section can make a trip possible within a very short period of time.

Firstly, let's reword this question to: "How can I spend 6 months on a luxurious yacht?" and "How can I travel on a luxurious yacht for cheap?" The answer to these questions can be, "I can rent a yacht for 6 months. It will cost only $20,000" and "I can share the expenses with 9 people who also want to travel the world on the luxurious yacht."

Secondly, let's break the task into 2 smaller pieces: "Where can I find 9 people who want to travel on a luxurious yacht?" and "How can I save $2,000 for the trip?" Both of these tasks are much more feasible than earning $200,000 but lead you to fulfillment of the same dream.

Albert Einstein said, "The formulation of a problem is often more essential than its solution, which may be merely a matter of mathematical or experimental skills. To raise new questions … requires creative imagination and makes real advances."

If you can't find a solution for a business task, it's very likely that you are simply asking the wrong question. Change the questions you are thinking about, change the abstraction level and break big problems into pieces. If you apply these techniques regularly, you will soon realize that you can solve problems of any difficulty.

Think and Rest

Think and Rest technique

During a summer between high school and university, I learned that a Cisco Certified Internetwork Expert (CCIE) is the most prestigious IT certification in the world. My dad said, "Andrii, there are only a few dozen CCIEs in all of the ex-USSR countries, they earn six-figure salaries and companies fight to get them hired." I set the goal, "I will become a CCIE no matter what."

In 2 years, I passed the CCIE written exam and the only thing that separated me and my dream was the CCIE lab part of the exam. To pass it you needed to configure a rack with 16 network devices according to the scenario presented.

I asked several Internetwork Experts, "How did you manage to get access to equipment worth $20,000 to prepare for the CCIE lab exam?" and received two types of answers: "The company I worked at provided access to the equipment" and "I spent my own money on access to a remote rack with equipment."

In 3 months I realized, "Not a single company in the Ukraine wants to hire an 18-year-old part-time for enough money to prepare for the CCIE lab." A friend who worked for the Cisco local distributor arranged for me to use some equipment, but after only 2 days of my practice it had been sold. I thought, "I tried all approaches that worked for others in the past and failed. It's a dead end."

In my case there was no reasonable way to get access to the expensive equipment. One day I visited the websites of all the companies that dealt with Cisco certifications, found email addresses of the CEOs and wrote the following letter, "Hi, I am 18 years old and have already passed the written part of the CCIE exam. If you can provide me access to the equipment necessary to prepare for the CCIE lab part of the exam, I am ready to do any work for you in exchange. You will also be able to say in your promotional materials that the youngest CCIE in Europe has gained the certification with the help of your company."

Looking back, I think that sending out that email was crazy, unreasonable and unprofessional. Who knew that one company would offer me a job to help improve their testing materials in exchange for money, and another would offer to have me write a brochure in exchange for equipment access during the time slots that were not sold to paying customers.

At 19, I passed the lab exam in Brussels, became the youngest CCIE in Europe and received a job offer from the Cisco office in the Ukraine. I attribute this success to an unconventional idea that allowed me to get access to expensive equipment and I attribute this idea to the Think and Rest technique that allowed me to generate it.

If you asked me, "Andrii, what is the most effective thinking strategy to produce high-quality business ideas?" I would certainly say, "Of, course Think and Rest." Think and Rest is an incredibly effective thinking technique that will allow you to produce successful business ideas with little effort.

Firstly, think about the problem you want to solve as hard as you can for 30 minutes, 60 minutes or several hours and write down all the ideas that come to your head, no matter how crazy. During this initial thinking stage you not only generate ideas but also let your subconscious mind know which ideas you need. If your problem is simple, you may find a good solution already during this initial brainstorming session, but if you didn't find an appropriate solution within the first several hours, forget about your problem completely and get back to your everyday life.

Secondly, after you stop thinking about the problem consciously, the subconscious will continue thinking about it 24/7. Your super-fast creative mind will process millions of thoughts and give you ideas while you are on a walk, taking a shower or sleeping. The subconscious mind is responsible for most original and successful ideas that you create. Once the subconscious generates an idea for you, write it down no matter where you are and what time of the day it is.

Finally, think about your task occasionally for 2 to 5 minutes. During this time you will not only generate fresh ideas but will also reactivate your creative mind and make it think intensively while you are not consciously thinking about the problem.

The Think and Rest technique will help you generate successful business ideas in 100% of cases. If after using this technique a great idea didn't come to you, it means that either not enough time has passed or that you don't have enough raw materials to create an idea from and need to do more research.

Think and Rest is a strategy that most effectively activates the thinking process in the brain. To become as effective at generating successful business ideas as possible, use Think and Rest consciously. The best innovators and thinkers in the world use this strategy daily.

Incubation period

If after a period of intense thinking you didn't generate an excellent idea, forget about the problem and switch to a completely different activity. Your analytical brain has set a program for your creative brain, which will continue thinking about the problem 24/7 in the back of your mind.

During the time when you don't consciously focus on the problem, the creative brain makes random connections between millions of thoughts in the back of your mind, and once it sees that one of the connections seems interesting it says, "Eureka! Here is an interesting idea." The more time your subconscious mind thinks about a problem, the more connections it makes and the higher the probability that a successful business idea will be generated.

A majority of scientists and entrepreneurs reported that they got their best ideas and insights while not actively thinking about the problem. The best ideas come when you forget about the problem and least expect them: while traveling, shaving, taking a shower, standing in line, jogging, talking to a friend, watching a play at the theater or sleeping.

When after an initial brainstorming session the flow of ideas dries up, get back to your everyday life. To keep the creative brain active, let it know that you still need ideas by occasionally thinking about the problem for few minutes from time to time. Great innovators are producing successful business ideas not because they work harder than others, but because they use an effective thinking process. Although the work that the subconscious mind does during the incubation period is invisible, it is the most essential part of this process.

C.G. Suits, the legendary Chief Scientist at General Electric, said: "All the discoveries in research laboratories came as hunches during a period of relaxation, following a period of intensive thinking and fact gathering."

Bertrand Russell, the British logician and mathematician, said: "I have found, for example, that if I have to write upon some rather difficult topic, the best plan is to think about it with very great intensity – the greatest intensity of which I am capable – for a few hours or days, and at the end of that time give orders, so to speak (to my subconscious mind) that the work is to proceed underground. After some months I return consciously to the topic and find that the work has been done."

When Carl Sagan, the American astronomer, got stuck on one project he moved to another one, allowing his subconscious to do the work. He wrote: "When you come back, you find to your amazement, nine times out of ten, that you have solved your problem – or your unconscious has – without you even knowing it."

Think about different problems simultaneously

Many years ago at the age of 14 I was sitting in a room full of tenth-graders waiting for a math competition to begin. If you were in the room with me you would have heard the lady say: "You will have 4 hours to solve 4 problems. I will collect your papers promptly at the end of the contest. Now you can turn over your sheets with problem descriptions and begin. Good luck!"

After 60 minutes of thinking about the first problem, I thought, "I still haven't made any progress. If I spend as much time on all the other problems and make as much progress, I will definitely lose the competition. Let's see what the other problems are like."

I spent 10 minutes on problem number 2, made a little bit of progress, got stuck and moved on to problem number 3. After 20 minutes, I solved it. I thought, "Wow! Let's see what I can do with problem number 4." In 10 minutes after having thought about problem 4, I got stuck and moved back to problem number 1. After 15 minutes of thinking I made some more progress, got stuck again and moved to problem number 2. In 25 minutes I finally solved problem number 2. I was switching between the remaining problems over and over again until the end of the contest, and by the time the lady was collecting the papers I had solved 3 problems.

I became the second-place winner and received the right to represent my city at the country level math competition. But perhaps the most valuable prize I received was an invaluable lesson that helped me to generate ideas more effectively not only at school but also in adult life. "If you switch between problems, your subconscious will think about them simultaneously and your productivity at producing ideas will increase several times."

The creativity researcher Mihaly Csikszentmihalyi interviewed 96 exceptional scientists, artists and writers and realized that all of them worked on more than one project at a time. If you switch between several problems, your subconscious will think about all of them in the back of your mind while you work, rest and sleep, and you will generate many more great ideas at the same time. Working on several problems simultaneously is one of the most powerful creativity techniques and will significantly increase productivity of your subconscious mind during the incubation period.

Think in pictures

When my wife, Olena, began learning English, I realized that she speaks extremely slowly. I asked, "Olena, why is it when you want to say something you first make a huge pause and then slowly say one word after another?"

"Well, I first decide what I want to say in Russian, translate a sentence into English and then say it aloud."

"Olena, do you know how children learn to speak? A mother shows an orange to a child and says, 'It is orange.' Then she points at the house and says, 'It's a house.' After a while, a child associates in his or her mind a picture of an orange with the word 'orange' and a picture of the house with the word 'house.' If you want to speak quickly, you need to associate pictures of the objects and actions directly with English words and avoid making a translation in your mind. An analytical brain is responsible for translating and it significantly slows down a process of turning a thought into a sentence."

The same happens in your thinking about business ideas. If you try to talk to yourself or think using words, the conscious brain is activated, your thinking slows down millions of times and your chances of creating interesting ideas become very slim.

Albert Einstein, Thomas Edison and Henry Ford left enormous amounts of diagrams and pictures in their notebooks. One of the reasons why they were extremely successful idea creators was their habit of thinking visually. Albert Einstein said that he rarely thought in words. Thoughts came to him in images and only then did he express them with words and formulas.

Imagine a "car" and a "soap." Now, create several combinations of these objects to generate new ideas. You might say, "A soap that is in the form of a car, a car seat that is in the form of a soap, car washing using soap, a car that uses soap instead of fuel." But before you say all these ideas you may first imagine them in your head.

Remember that your super-fast subconscious mind thinks using pictures, and if you want to be effective at generating business ideas, you should think using pictures rather than words. Great ideas are first created as images in your head and only then described using words.

Quantity over quality of ideas

Avoid making decisions based on past experience

While studying at Yale University, Fred Smith wrote a paper in which he described a concept of Federal Express. His management professor gave him a "C" for the project and said, "The concept is interesting and well-formed, but in order to earn better than a 'C', the idea must be feasible." Once Fred founded FedEx, almost every delivery expert in the United States predicted that his company would fail based on their experience in the industry. They said that no one would pay a premium price for speed and reliability.

We are used to making decisions based on our past experience because in the majority of situations it's reasonable and helps avoid making the same mistake twice. If, however, you take into consideration only what worked in the past, you may come to the same old ideas. If you want to create successful business ideas, you need to tell the world what will work in the future, not what worked in the past.

Several years ago while studying how the brain works, I stumbled upon a very interesting statistic that said, "When you do kickboxing, your body burns about 10 calories per minute; when you walk, your body burns about 4 calories per minute; the brain on its own burns only about one tenth of a calorie per minute. However, when you actively think, the brain burns 1.5 calories per minute." Taking into account that the brain makes up only 2 percent of the body weight, that's a huge amount of energy!

Your brain always tries to conserve as much energy as possible. Once you begin thinking about any task, the brain quickly scans memory for past experiences and in a few seconds says: "Here is a solution." You say, "Hey, brain, I don't like this one. Give me another one." The brain looks into the past experiences and again in a few seconds says, "Here is a solution." Unfortunately, these solutions are often obvious and of little value for making a business successful.

Tell your friends, "Please write down a list of 20 animals." At the beginning, they will most probably list such animals as "cat," "dog," "bear" or "lion." These animals are freshest in your friends' memory, because they often see them on the street, in the zoo, on TV or in advertisements. At the end of the list there will be more rare animals such as "puma," "sloth" or "guinea pig."

Research shows that we recall common objects faster than less typical ones. Research also shows that when thinking about a problem, the brain tends to give most typical solutions based on past experience faster than original and creative solutions.

Your brain will avoid thinking really hard until it runs out of quick solutions based on your experience of what worked in the past. The only way to make the brain think hard and produce world-class ideas is to make it generate a lot of ideas.

The greatest innovators know this and when they think on a problem they are never satisfied with the first or second solution that comes to their head. They generate all the ideas they can and then pick the most promising ones. Einstein was once asked how his thinking was different from the thinking of the average person. He said, "When searching for a needle in a haystack, other people quit when they find a needle. I look for what other needles might be in the haystack."

Quantity equals quality

Imagine that you want to solve a particular problem and need one perfect solution. Many people would say, "Yeah, I will think until I find the perfect solution. Once I find it, I will stop thinking." Although this approach seems intuitive, it rarely works. Why? Let's review the thinking strategies of the left and right brain.

The left brain looks for one and the best solution for the problem. In everyday life, we use the left brain in a majority of cases and it gives us a good answer. You ask, "Which route should I choose to get to work? Is this coat expensive? In what year did the Second World War begin?" The left brain quickly looks at what worked in the past and answers, "Here is your best answer." We are so used to using the logical left brain every day that we try to use it even when we need a creative new solution. Unfortunately, the logical brain is not only useless for generating creative ideas, but is even harmful because it blocks the creative right brain.

The right brain is millions of times faster than the left logical brain and is responsible for generating creative and original ideas. The creative brain looks for many solutions for the same problem. Even though you may eventually implement only one solution, during the idea generation stage think about all possible and impossible solutions. The more ideas you create, the better your final solution will be.

Professor Dean Keith decided to explore the relationship between the quantity and quality of ideas. He studied the work of hundreds of the most creative scientists and made a very interesting discovery. The best scientists created more successful ideas than the mediocre ones. However, the best scientists also created many more bad ideas than the mediocre scientists.

The vast majority of papers written by the world's most famous scientists were never cited. A small percentage of them received a little over 100 citations and only several papers had an incredible impact on the world.

Professor Keith has done the same study with composers and other fine artists and found that the more bad ideas a composer, a scientist or an artist generated, the more successful ideas he or she had.

Thomas Edison filed over 2,000 patents, but the majority of them didn't make him a cent. Albert Einstein published over 300 scientific papers, but the majority of them are not cited by other scientists. Pablo Picasso created more than 20,000 pieces of art, but most of them are not presented at the best art exhibitions. There is a direct correlation between quantity and quality of ideas. The majority of ideas that the best ideas creators generate are bad, some of them are average and very few are genius. These few genius ideas make the best creators enormously successful.

Nature creates multiple species through blind trial and error and lets the process of natural selection decide which species survive. In nature, 95% of new species fail and die. Those species that survive, thrive and become part of the world's ecosystem. As an ideas generator, you need to generate a large quantity of ideas and give them a chance to live. A few of these ideas will survive and make your business incredibly successful. The more ideas you generate the more likely one of them will be a treasure. To become a world-class ideas creator, remember the most important equation in creativity: quantity equals quality.

Set ideas quota

Several years ago, I conducted a workshop, at a famous international company, about generating business ideas. I split the participants into groups and gave them a task, "Please come up with 100 applications of the brick. Your ideas can be crazy or unrealistic, but by all means meet the quantity requirement. You have 30 minutes, go!"

If you received such a task, at first you would quickly write down applications of the brick from your past experience. For example, "A brick can be used for building a house or a brick can be used as a weapon." In a few minutes the typical applications of the brick you can recall from your past experience end and this is the time when the brain begins really thinking.

For example, the ideas you might have will be something like, "A brick can be used as a musical instrument, as a toy and as a fan." You will realize that indeed creative and valuable ideas come after you have exhausted the most obvious ideas from your memory and lie somewhere between number 80 and number 100.

After the exercise with a brick, I gave participants another task, "Please come up with 200 headlines for the upcoming advertising campaign of the company's product. Your ideas can be crazy or unrealistic, but by all means meet the quantity requirement. You have 60 minutes, go!" If you are curious to know how the workshop participants finished the task, I will tell you. All groups came up with more than 200 ideas. Some of the ideas were extremely interesting and the company implemented one of them.

During a brainstorming session, set a goal to generate a large quantity of ideas within a short period of time. Put your internal critic on hold and let your imagination generate enough ideas, no matter how crazy, silly or unrealistic, to meet the quota. The first third of ideas will be old ideas from past experience, the second half will be more interesting ideas and the final third will most likely have exceptional ideas that will make your business successful. The ideas quota technique forces the creative brain to think, generate a large quantity of ideas, and later select the most promising among them.

The takeaway message from this section can be excellently summarized by the words of the international design firm IDEO founder David Kelley: "If you're forced to come up with ten things, it's the clichéd things that you have off the top of your head. But if you have to come up with a hundred, it forces you to go beyond the clichés."

Set constraints and think inside the box

One Monday when I was 12 years old, a teacher gave us homework. She said, "Please write an essay on any topic." In 3 days, my friend Max went to the teacher and said, "I was thinking hard for hours, but still don't have any ideas. I can't write even one line." The teacher asked, "Max, where do you live?" He said, "I live across the street from the theater." The teacher said, "Well, please write an essay about the left wing of the theater in front of your house." Max went home and wrote a 10-page essay in the afternoon. His essay was the best in class. Now Max is a director at an international creative agency and generating ideas is his everyday work.

In creativity there is nothing more paralyzing than the task to create anything you want with all the resources you need. Suppose you say, "I want to generate any business ideas. I have an unlimited amount of time and money for the project." That just kills creativity and you will be very unlikely to generate really good ideas. However, if you define how many ideas you want to generate, set a deadline, limit the budget for the project, and describe a task for your subconscious as specifically as possible, you will generate many outstanding ideas, some of which will eventually become successful businesses. Well-defined problems with a deadline, ideas quota and resources limitation have much more chance of being solved creatively.

Don't assume fake constraints for your task, however. If a solution didn't work in the past, it doesn't mean that it won't work this time. If experts say that an idea is bad, it certainly needs consideration. If this is how things always worked here, challenge it.

The best idea creators know: To generate a successful idea, you need to give the subconscious full freedom and generate many ideas, no matter how crazy, controversial or unrealistic. However, to be able to generate them you need to give your brain a direction: define an idea quota, deadline, resources and most importantly describe a task as specifically as possible. Your subconscious will generate amazing ideas for you, but before generating them it needs to know exactly what you want.

Essence of ideas

Lesson from the Market

Imagine that you live in a world where the success of each business is determined by an old and very wise man, whose name is Market. There is always a huge line of people, in front of his house, who want to hear his verdict about their business ideas. If Market says, "Your idea is excellent," then your product will be a big success; if Market says, "This idea isn't good," your product won't be in demand.

One day a young man came to Market and said, "I lived on an uninhabited island all my life and have never heard the ideas of others so you can be sure that my product is original. I spent 10 years on creating an original idea that can have a big impact on mankind and after many failures invented a wheel."

Market looked at the young man and smiled, "Young man, this idea isn't good. The wheel was invented thousands of years ago and people already use it in cars, bicycles, trains, buses and even airplanes."

Young man: "But, Market, I didn't know that the wheel was already invented. I created it completely independently. I can't believe that 10 years of my work are wasted."

Market said, "Young man, I see so many people who come to me with the hope of becoming successful but get disappointed just like you. Stay in my house as long as you want and observe which products I approve. If you are attentive enough, the next idea you bring will be a huge success."

Next in line was Steve Jobs. Market said, "Hi, Steve. What have you brought to me this time?"

"Market, I observed that when people unintentionally pull the power cord of the computer, it falls down and gets damaged. I want to solve this problem by creating a magnet that connects the computer to the power cord. When you abruptly pull the power cord the magnet will disconnect and the computer will be safe."

"Your idea is excellent, Steve." said Market.

The young man asked, "Market, I just talked with a woman from Japan and she said that in her country rice cookers with magnetic latches that prevent a spill have already been produced for many years. Steve's idea isn't original. Why did you approve it?"

"Young man, I don't care if an idea is fully original. People copy and build up on ideas of others every day. This is how progress in society is made. The only thing I care about is that your product is the best among those that are brought to me and that it can change the lives of people for the better. Steve's idea improves the experience of the laptop users and will be successful."

The young man carefully observed which ideas Market approved and by the end of the day asked, "Market, I see that among ideas that you approved were MTV, drive-thru banking and rollerblading. I learned that these ideas are a combination of the old ones. For example: MTV is a combination of music and television, drive-thru banking is a combination of a car and banking and rollerblading is a combination of ice skating and roller skating. These products aren't fully original, why did you let them be successful?"

"You see, young man, there is no such thing as an original idea. All ideas are either modifications or combinations of the old ones. The more old ideas you learn, the more material you have for creating your own ideas. I don't care how original your idea is, the only thing I care about is that your product makes the lives of other people better. Before you leave, please tell me what you learned today."

"Market, I learned that each idea is either a modification or combination of the old ones. I decided to learn as many ideas of others as I can to later adopt or combine them for creating my own successful products. However, the most important thing I learned is that successful ideas make people's lives better."

Market looked at the young man, winked and said, "I think that we will see each other often. I am looking forward to hearing your next idea."

Combine ideas

Make connections

When I studied at the University of Michigan, one day I asked my friend Martin, "Hey, Martin, how was your summer internship?" He said, "Andrii, I worked in a supply chain department of a large medical equipment producer. I have developed a new ordering strategy which saves the company over $10M per year. The company issued me a job offer and as a token of appreciation will pay for my education."

I asked, "Martin, how did you manage to get this idea?"

"Well, Andrii, actually I just brought directors of all the company divisions to the same room and asked how they place their orders now. We have taken the best ideas from all existing strategies and based on them, created a strategy that is a company-wide standard today."

Creativity researchers have discovered that all great ideas are combinations or modifications of the existing ones. Geniuses create their breakthrough inventions by making connections between existing ideas, just like Martin during his summer internship. Henry Ford once said, "The simple secret of my genius is that I created something new out of the ideas and inventions of others." Steve Jobs said, "When you ask creative people how they did something, they feel a little guilty because they didn't really do it; they just saw something. It seemed obvious to them after a while. That's because they were able to connect experiences they've had and synthesize new things." American advertising executive Jerry Della Femina said: "Creativity is about making a lot of quick connections — about the things you know, the things you've seen. The more you've done, the easier it is to make that jump."

Professor Dean Keith, in his research, found that creative geniuses generate more breakthrough ideas than other people. What he also found is that they generate many more useless and unsuccessful ideas. The creation of a breakthrough business idea depends on chance and geniuses increase its probability by making a lot of connections between random thoughts, experiences and ideas.

If you want to dramatically increase your effectiveness in producing great business ideas, make this your invocation: "All ideas are a combination or modification of existing ideas. To increase the probability of creating a successful business idea, I will make more random combinations between thoughts, experiences and ideas every day."

Just focus your attention and think

When I studied at elementary school, our teacher once said, "Don't think about a yellow monkey." The entire class laughed because we all thought about the yellow monkey. In my imagination the monkey was sitting on a bench, then dancing and eventually sitting at the desk.

When you concentrate your attention on a particular object or a problem, after some time your brain will get bored and begin thinking about how to perceive it differently, decompose it into parts or connect with other thoughts, experiences or ideas. I am often asked, "Andrii, how should I be thinking?" and I answer, "Simply focus your attention on the problem and your creative mind will do the rest."

Leonardo da Vinci discovered that the human brain can't concentrate deliberately on two ideas no matter how different without forming connections between them, eventually.

Psychologists have discovered that our brain always tries to find patterns and sense in everything. If you concentrate on two absolutely dissimilar concepts, eventually the brain will build connections between them in order to make them a combination that makes sense. For example, if you think about a donkey and TV, your brain may generate the following ideas: a cartoon about a donkey, a TV in the form of a donkey, a donkey that carries TVs on its back, a TV producer logo in the form of donkey or a TV channel about donkeys.

When you want to generate a successful business idea, simply concentrate your attention on your problem and a random idea. The subconscious mind will deal with creating combinations and modifications. The more random ideas and thoughts your brain combines with your problem, the more chance you have of coming up with a really brilliant idea.

Exercise: Random objects

"Random objects" will develop your habit of combining seemingly unrelated objects to create new business ideas. The way you will generate ideas in this exercise is very similar to how business geniuses produce their best ideas.

Pick two random unrelated objects and make a connection between them in order to create a new product or a new business idea. Within 5 minutes generate as many combinations as possible and write them down. Don't try to make your ideas realistic, try to generate as many ideas as possible, no matter how crazy. You will always be able to think about how to make some of these ideas a reality and choose the most viable one later, however at this stage let your subconscious generate combinations without any limitations.

For example, if you pick soap and a car, the combinations may be: car in the form of a soap, use soap to wash a car, a car seat in the form of a soap, a bathroom in a car, soap used as a fuel instead of gasoline or a car that sprinkles soap on a street to wash it.

Do you see how this exercise can be applied in generating successful business ideas? Imagine that one object is a question you want to solve and a second object is a random item or idea. Do this exercise with many random items and ideas and eventually you will find a genius solution for your task. This is exactly the process that the world's best innovators use. Successful ideas are combinations of other ideas. And the most effective way to generate them is to make many combinations of random ideas. The more connections you make, the more likely you are to generate a successful idea.

When a chef wants to create a new, delicious dish he or she takes different ingredients from the refrigerator and combines or modifies them with a knife, a mixer or a cooker. The more a chef experiments, the higher are the chances to create a tasty original dish. In business, ingredients are ideas and life experiences that are stored in your memory. To create new combinations among the ideas (ingredients), instead of kitchen appliances, you use your subconscious mind. If you make it a habit to regularly focus attention on your task and random ideas, concepts and thoughts, your brain will generate a lot of ideas, some of which will make your business enormously successful.

Copy ideas

Before 1981 when Jack Welch became CEO of GE, the company was resistant to ideas or products "not invented here" and concentrated on creating all ideas within the organization's boundaries. Jack set a new vision, "Someone, somewhere has a better idea" and happily adapted these ideas for specific needs of the company. Within the next 20 years, GE's value rose 4,000% and Jack Welch was called CEO of the Century by Forbes magazine. In a documentary he said, "It's a badge of honor to have found from Motorola a quality program, from HP a product development program, from Toyota an asset management system."

No matter how clever you are, no matter how purposeful you are, you will never be able to create more ideas than thousands of geniuses before you. If you want to become a successful business ideas creator, first you need to learn how to copy and then how to innovate on top of existing ideas. If you created an outstanding idea but later realized that it was created by someone in the past, you have wasted your time. Why? You could have copied and applied this idea to your business and spent time on creating new ideas on top of existing ideas. Your customers don't care who has created an idea, the only thing they care about is who has the best product and service on the market.

Do you know why ideas are not copyrightable? Because copying is how progress is made. All innovators copy ideas from each other and innovate on top of them. Imagine that the idea of producing a computer was owned by one company. If it were so, computers today would probably be extremely expensive and far less advanced.

The USA built its economy during the industrial revolution by copying ideas and technologies from Europe and later innovating on top of them. Japan built its prospering economy after World War II by imitating and copying U.S. and European technologies. Since the 1990s, China has been actively copying ideas and technologies from the USA, Europe and Japan and its economy is rapidly growing.

Innovations and business ideas depend on the exchange of ideas. New ideas are combinations or modifications of existing ideas. The more life experiences you have, the more ideas of others you know, the better ideas you will be able to build on top of them. With the development of the internet and cheap transportation, you have access to billions of ideas around the world. Learn them, copy them, modify them and you will be able to multiply many times your effectiveness at producing successful business ideas.

Very often people fall into the trap of thinking that the ideas they produce should be completely original, and significantly limit their creative productivity. Don't be one of them. If you realize that completely original ideas do not exist, stop trying to create something out of nothing and expose yourself as much as possible to ideas of others, you will increase your creative productivity many times.

Most everything I've done I've copied from somebody else. – Sam Walton

Good artists copy, great artists steal. – Pablo Picasso

We have always been shameless about stealing great ideas. – Steve Jobs

When people call something "original," nine out of ten times they just don't know the references or the original sources involved. What a good artist understands is that nothing comes from nowhere. All creative work builds on what came before. Nothing is completely original. – Jonathan Lethem

Don't strive to create the most original ideas, strive to create the best products and services on the market. Learn and copy great ideas as much as possible. It is essential for creating excellent ideas and your success in business.

Adopt ideas

My friend Dmitriy from the Ukraine told a story about how his mother became successful in business. In the 1990s, Dmitriy's mother Irina had a dream to open a pharmacy and mortgaged her apartment to purchase a stock of pharmaceuticals. Irina was selling them in a kiosk until she saved enough money to open a pharmacy. Irina went to Germany for 2 weeks and visited hundreds of pharmacies around the country. She observed how pharmacies operate in Germany and wrote down all the interesting ideas she noticed.

After coming home, Irina adopted these ideas to the Ukrainian market and implemented them in her own pharmacy. After a few months it became the best and most popular pharmacy in the town. Now she owns over 20 pharmacies, lives in a huge house and is a multimillionaire.

Thomas Edison, one of the greatest inventors of the 20th century, believed that seeing analogies is key to creating successful ideas. He said, "Make it a habit to keep on the lookout for novel and interesting ideas that others have used successfully. Your idea needs to be original only in its adaptation to the problem you are working on."

One of the most popular TV shows in the Ukraine is *Ukraine's Got Talent*. In this show, amateur or unknown performers show their talents on stage. They are judged by 3 celebrities and the audience votes. The final show of the first season was watched by 18.6 million people, which is more than 40% of Ukraine's population. Do Ukrainians care that the format of the show was copied and adopted from *America's Got Talent* and *Britain's Got Talent*? No, the only thing they care is that it is very interesting to watch.

Constantly think about how good ideas can be adopted from other countries, other businesses or products. Irina's story isn't unique; enormous fortunes have been made by adopting existing ideas.

Early adopters win

In 2004, Mark Zuckerberg, then a student at Harvard University, developed and launched Facebook social network. Facebook became a multibillion-dollar company and the most popular social network in the world with over 750 million active users in 2010.

In 2006, having just graduated from St. Petersburg State University, Pavel Durov adopted the idea of Facebook for Russian-speaking countries and launched Vkontakte social network. In 2012 Vkontakte became the 19th most visited website in the world and the 2nd most popular social network in Europe.

Technically, a social network isn't difficult to develop. In fact, today you can create your own social network in a matter of minutes even if you don't know how to code. Many thousands of people worldwide copied the idea of Facebook and launched their own social networks, very few of which became popular. You might ask, "What is the difference between Pavel Durov and thousands of other people who launched their social networks but failed to make them successful?"

Pavel Durov was one of the first users of Facebook. He noticed the potential of the social network idea far before Facebook became known by millions of people around the world. In 2008, many of my friends in the Ukraine became users of Facebook and Vkontakte almost simultaneously. Today they get invited to some newly created social networks almost every month but don't join them. Why? Firstly, because they want to be members of the biggest social networks and secondly because they can't actively participate in more than 2-3 social networks.

Constantly look for emerging business ideas; once they turn into billion-dollar businesses it might be too late to develop a successful business by adopting them. You will have the biggest benefit of copying them if you notice their potential earlier than the rest of the world. Become an early adopter of new services and products at the stage when they are only on the way to being widely used. The earlier you see a potential in a particular idea, the more value you will get from adopting it in your own business.

The same ideas may come to the minds of many people, however if you get the idea earlier than others, implement it earlier and promote it earlier, you will have a significant advantage. Timing is very critical for the success of your ideas. Spot opportunities early because early adopters win.

Think differently

On the opening day of *The Hunger Games* movie, my wife and I were looking for a parking spot in front of the cinema in Santa Clara, CA. It was dark, it was raining and the parking lot was fully packed with cars. There was obviously not a single spot available, however we hoped that somebody would be leaving the parking lot and we could take the space.

In 15 minutes Olena said, "There are dozens of cars besides us circling the parking lot and even if some space frees up, it will be taken in a heartbeat." I thought, "We should either go home or think differently from everybody else. What place would nobody consider for parking?"

In a few minutes, an idea came to my head, we drove away from the main entrance, turned and found that almost all the parking spots at the back of the cinema were free. I parked the car. Within 2 minutes, we walked to the main entrance and enjoyed the excellent movie.

The market is like a big parking lot. If you are doing what everybody else is doing, it will be very difficult to compete and build a profitable business. When you think about the problem, consider what ideas you created, what competitors are doing and then change the direction of your thinking. To create successful ideas and find profitable business niches, challenge the status quo, look at the problem from different angles and make it your mantra: "Think differently."

Raw materials for ideas

Why you need raw materials

When I was 15, my family moved and during my last year before college I went to a high school which was not only closer to my house, but also significantly stronger in math.

I approached my new math teacher, Alexander, and said, "Alexander, I want to achieve the maximum I can in competitive math and I am willing to work as hard as possible this year. I know that you prepared several international level math Olympiad winners. Please suggest what I can work on at home in addition to regular classes."

He said, "You see, Andrii, to win a math Olympiad, relying only on agility of the brain isn't enough. You should also rely on your competitive math experience.

"I will give you books with collections of problems from past national and international math competitions. Think about each problem yourself for some time, and then read the solution in the back of the book. After a while, you will notice patterns and memorize various approaches for tackling problems. The more solutions of others you read, the more approaches for solving problems are in your arsenal and the more likely you are to solve a math problem.

"Once you face a problem in a math competition, you will have many different approaches in your arsenal to begin solving it and coupled with agility of the brain you will become a very strong contestant who can win."

A new idea is a modification or combination of old ones. Old ideas are a raw material for creative thinking. The more ideas of other people you know, the more connections your brain will be able to make and the more likely you are to create an interesting and valuable business idea.

Expose yourself to new experiences

One day little Jimmy went to his best friend Suzy's house and noticed what beautiful constructions she built from a Lego set. He looked at cars, ships and castles and decided, "I want to build beautiful Lego constructions, too."

Jimmy took two little pieces of a Lego set that he owned. He spent hours looking at them and trying to put them together in all possible combinations but realized that no matter what he did these 2 pieces never looked like a car, a ship or a castle. He went to Suzy and said, "Suzy, I am just not creative enough to build beautiful Lego constructions." Suzy looked at him, smiled and said, "Jimmy, you are more than talented for creating beautiful Lego constructions. You just don't have enough constructor pieces. I have been collecting my Lego pieces for years and now have thousands of them. If you had as many pieces as I do, you would easily create even better constructions."

Ideas are combinations of other ideas and the more diverse life experiences you have, the more different ideas you will be able to construct. Many people say, "I can't create great business ideas. I am not creative." However, the true reason why they fail is that they have too few different experiences in their memory to construct new ideas from.

The world's greatest thinkers have an insatiable curiosity and actively seek new experiences that can increase the amount of their creative constructor pieces. They travel, make new acquaintances, try various hobbies, attend conferences and seminars, and read books, magazines and blogs.

People whose life follows the same pattern for years may find themselves in a situation like little Jimmy who tried to create something incredible from just several pieces of a Lego set. Constantly bombard your brain with new ideas and experiences which will become raw materials for your future successful business ideas. The more different experiences you have had in life, the more ideas of others you have learned, the more creative combinations your brain will be able to make and the more valuable ideas it will generate. If you want to be a world-class thinker, a quest for new creative raw materials should become your habit.

Creativity is just connecting things. When you ask creative people how they did something, they feel a little guilty because they didn't really do it, they just saw something. It seemed obvious to them after a while. That's because they were able to connect experiences they've had and synthesize new things. And the reason they were able to do that was that they've had more experiences or they have thought more about their experiences than other people. Unfortunately, that's too rare a commodity. A lot of people in our industry haven't had very diverse experiences. So they don't have enough dots to connect, and they end up with very linear solutions without a broad perspective on the problem. – Steve Jobs

Write ideas down

When I studied at school, my math teacher kept repeating, "If you haven't written down a solution for the problem, you haven't solved a problem." Before I took this advice seriously, quite often I had to say, "I solved this problem yesterday, but just forgot the solution."

If there was just one tip I could give, that would help you the most in creating successful business ideas, it would be this: "Always write down your ideas! Write each idea down as soon as it comes to your head or they will go as quickly as they came. Write down the idea no matter when and where it came." Capturing ideas has several benefits:

Firstly, the ideas are saved and can be used later. For any successful business ideas creator, not writing down an idea looks even more ridiculous than burning $100 bills with a lighter. Ideas are treasures and should always be saved.

Secondly, writing down an idea sends a signal to your subconscious mind, "Thank you very much for generating this wonderful idea. I highly appreciate what you do for me. Please generate more ideas." If the subconscious mind feels appreciated, it will work harder and generate even more wonderful ideas for you. Imagine that you say something to your friend, and he or she doesn't listen. You repeat a second time but he or she doesn't care about what you say again. Eventually you stop talking. The same happens with your right brain if you don't appreciate ideas that it generates.

Finally, when you have many ideas on paper you can easily switch between them. Each idea can be modified or combined with other ideas to create new ideas. For example when Edison's Ore Milling Company proved to be financially unprofitable, he looked through his notebooks with ideas. Edison figured out that his company had a very similar business model to one in the cement industry and formed Edison Portland Cement in 1899.

Thomas Edison, Benjamin Franklin, Leonardo da Vinci, the Wright brothers, Virginia Woolf, Carl Jung, Charles Darwin and thousands of other famous entrepreneurs, innovators, writers, scientists and artists carried notebooks and wrote down all their ideas. This habit played an important role in their success.

What to do if the idea caught you off guard?

Imagine that just before you fall asleep an amazing idea comes to your head. You might think, "I am too tired to write down the idea. I will do it first thing in the morning." Guess what, once you wake up the idea will be gone and may never come to you again.

The best ideas often come when you least expect them: in a grocery store, while you exercise in the gym or sleep. Although, writing down an idea often may seem terribly inconvenient, always write it down no matter when and where it came. If you got an idea at 3 in the morning, wake up and write it down. If you got an idea during an important business meeting, take a pen and write it down. If you got an idea in a grocery store, find a way to write it down. This habit will have an enormous impact on your success in business and life.

You might ask, "Andrii, what if there is no way for me to write down an idea? For example, I am driving a car or presenting in front of a large audience. Can I remember the idea to write it down later?"

One day I went jogging to the stadium and was thinking about what makes a book memorable and interesting to read. Three valuable ideas popped up in my head: "The text should be succinct. The book should have stories or at least metaphors. Knowing what to leave out is even more important than what to include in the book." I thought, "Hey, I have to either stop jogging and go home or remember the ideas for the next 45 minutes and write them down later."

Memory experts have discovered that people don't remember ideas or facts, they only remember pictures. So, if you want to remember an idea, you have to associate it with a picture in your imagination. I associated "succinct" with a "tennis ball," "leaving information out" with "throwing away trash" and "telling metaphors" with a wise man sitting in a lotus pose. I then combined 3 pictures into one: a wise man throwing away trash with his right hand and holding a tennis ball in his left hand. Using this technique I was able not only to recall and write down these 3 ideas in 45 minutes, but also to remember them even years after the day they came to me.

Businesses become enormously successful or go bankrupt because of great ideas or lack of them. Make it a habit to write down ideas as soon as they come into your head no matter what. Even if you are walking in a desert or running a marathon and there is no way to write down an idea immediately, associate it with a picture in your imagination to not let it go. Great idea creators say that writing down all their ideas was essential for the breakthroughs in business, science or art that they made. This habit will increase your productivity in creating high-quality business ideas multiple times and have an enormous impact on your success in life.

Beliefs of the world-class innovator

Belief and desire

Your subconscious mind is an incredibly powerful thinking mechanism that is programmed by your desires. The more you want to solve a particular task, the harder your subconscious will think to find a solution.

For example, if you say, "It would be nice to find a solution for my task" your subconscious would do nothing. If you say, "I really want to find a solution" your subconscious would think and give you some ideas. However, if you say, "I am obsessed with what I am doing and have a burning desire to find a solution" your subconscious will think at full capacity and generate a lot of high-quality ideas that will make your business successful.

The best business innovators know the secret of effective thinking and if you ask any of them about his or her success secret, the answer is always the same: "Do what you are passionate about." This advice is very simple and you may have heard it numerous times. Your success in generating ideas will depend on whether you act upon it or not.

Even if you have a burning desire to generate ideas you may block your subconscious by thinking, "I am not sure if I can generate good ideas," "I can't generate good ideas" or "I will see if I can generate good ideas or not." The most important belief of the great thinkers is "I will definitely find an excellent solution for my task." Your subconscious is very sensitive to your beliefs. If you doubt that you will generate great ideas, the subconscious will be blocked by your analytical brain. If you are 100% confident that you will generate great ideas, it will be unstoppable and excellent ideas will flow into your brain as quickly as possible.

When I asked my friend Max, who's been working over 10 years as a creative director in a world-famous company, what is most important for generating high-quality ideas he said, "Andrii, it is your 100% belief that you will generate them."

Remember the magic induction, "I have a burning desire to create successful business ideas and a 100% confidence that I will generate them." It turns ordinary people into the world's greatest thinkers.

Nothing great was ever accomplished without enthusiasm. – Ralph Waldo Emerson

It's very hard to succeed in something unless you take the first step – which is to become very interested in it. – Sir William Osler

Visualization

When I was 22, I had a burning desire to receive a Masters of Business Administration degree from one of the top 10 business schools in the USA. I realized, "The average candidate is 28 years old and has at least 5 years of experience in finance, supply chain management, marketing or strategy, which I don't. Basically my chances of getting accepted are slim."

I drew on an A4 sheet of paper a picture of where I was a student at one of the top 10 MBA schools and hung it on the wall near my desk. Every time I looked at it, I imagined that I had already been accepted and enjoyed my time in the MBA program. Within the next several months, I had generated numerous amazing ideas of how to increase my chances of getting accepted. And the miracle happened. I became the youngest student at the MBA program at Michigan Ross School of Business and even received a generous scholarship. Later, I learned that the reason I was accepted to one of the top 10 business schools was the law of attraction that successful idea generators have used for thousands of years. The law of attraction says, "You get what you think about, because your subconscious draws actions, thoughts and events to your life based on the program you set." Let's see how it works.

Every time you imagine that you already achieved a goal, your subconscious receives a task, "Please make my dream a reality." When you visualize your desire often, your creative brain thinks about potential ideas and solutions actively. Eventually you get necessary answers and make your dream a reality.

Draw a picture of your goal and hang it near your desk or bed. Every time you look at it imagine as vividly as possible that you have already achieved your dream. Your subconscious will get activated and will think about ways to make the picture from your imagination a reality. You can be sure that one day your goal will be achieved, no matter how big it is.

The law of attraction is one of the most effective techniques that exist not only for generating ideas but also for achieving goals. Use it for small goals that are achievable within a week, use it for average goals that are achievable within a month, and use it for huge strategic goals that you want to achieve within a decade. You can use the law of attraction as many times as you want and every time it will bring you whatever you ask for.

Visualization works perfectly in combination with the "Think and Rest" technique. Remember also that to make your subconscious think actively you need to have a burning desire to find a solution and a 100% confidence that you will generate great ideas.

Relocate to a high-performance state

One day, while a student at the University of Michigan, I went to a bar with my friends and several alumni to celebrate the end of the school year. After we ordered drinks and started a conversation, I said something funny and everybody laughed. I told another joke and everybody laughed, again. That afternoon the best comedians would have envied my ability to tell jokes on the spot, and for about 2 hours everyone was laughing really hard. I often struggle to come up with a great joke, but that afternoon I couldn't stop the flow of amazing jokes coming to my mind.

Do you remember a time when you were much more effective at generating ideas than usual? Researchers who model and replicate behavior of successful people found that the state we are in has a huge effect on our ability to generate ideas and we are most effective in a high-performance state.

In a high-performance state, people are relaxed, excited, lively, open and confident. The opposite is also true. If you become relaxed, excited, lively, open and confident simultaneously, you will get into the high-performance state and become dramatically more effective at producing ideas.

When actors play a role and want to convey a particular emotion of the character, they need to evoke it in themselves. They remember a situation from life when they felt this emotion clearly, relive it in their imagination and very soon begin to feel the emotion. This technique from the world of acting will help you with getting into a high-performance state.

To get into a high-performance state, you need to become simultaneously relaxed, excited, lively, open and confident. When these 5 states are combined, their individual effects on performance increase many times.

Relaxed

The more you relax, the more access you get to your creative brain and the more likely you are to generate successful business ideas. That's why we often come to original ideas while sleeping, taking a warm shower or meditating. A relaxed state is essential for activating the subconscious mind and being creative.

Relax all the muscles in your body completely except for the ones you need to stay upright. First, flex all your muscles and then quickly relax them. Relax all the muscles from your head to your feet. Pay attention to your breathing. Notice that each time you breathe and exhale, your body relaxes more and more until you are fully relaxed.

Excited

Imagine how awesome it will be when you have generated an excellent business idea. Imagine how your life will change, what you will be doing and what your relatives and friends will be telling you. Relieve your wonderful future in imagination and increase excitement until you feel as excited as a 5-year-old kid before getting a Christmas present.

Lively

Become energetic. Feel the power within you and your readiness to do something. To become energetic, jump, dance, do physical exercise or just remember how it felt when you did something active. If you imagine it clearly enough, your nervous system won't notice any difference. Remember, however, that you need to build up your energy while staying completely relaxed. As soon as you notice tension – relax yourself. It might seem impossible to be lively and relaxed simultaneously, but it is easy. It's an amazing feeling of outside calmness and internal readiness.

Open

Zen Buddhism has a concept of "beginner's mind." Zen teachers say that having a beginner's mind means facing life like a child, being full of curiosity, amazement and open to anything new. Openness is one of the foundations of creativity. Be open to all opportunities and ideas, no matter how crazy they look at first glance.

Remember a time when you were ready to accept anything that the world has to offer. You don't know what will happen in the next moment, but it is not important because you are ready to accept anything. Build up a feeling of openness until you can clearly feel it.

Confident

If you think that you are not creative or if you doubt that you can come up with an amazing idea, your subconscious will be blocked and will indeed not generate successful ideas. Being 100% confident that great ideas will come to you is one of the most important things in the idea generation process.

Recall a situation from your life when you felt absolutely confident in yourself. Maybe you said or did something you were 100% sure about. Relive it as clearly as you can and feel what you felt at that time. While building up a feeling of confidence, remain open, lively, excited and relaxed.

Again

Repeat again everything mentioned above! Every time you increase the intensity of each feeling, make sure you stay simultaneously relaxed, excited, lively, open and confident. Go through this list several times and very soon you will get into a high-productivity state.

A high-performance state is a state in which the creative brain works most effectively. I highly recommend getting into a high-performance state whenever you need to generate ideas. This state will do magic with your ability to create successful business ideas.

Generating ideas is a game

When I was about 12 years old, I had a huge fear. I was afraid of getting beaten up by bullies on the street. I was so scared to go to school every day that my parents put me into the Kiokushin Karate school to get this fear out of me.

Every training session, after stretching and practicing punches, we had practice fights. I was fighting against older, bigger and more experienced guys. It was painful, unpleasant and that time lasted an eternity for me.

One day our trainer, Alexander, said, "Everyone, please sit in a circle. I have to tell you something." What he said not only changed my attitude towards karate and fighting but also my attitude towards generating ideas.

"Guys, don't fear the pain from the punches. Have an attitude towards a fight as you would towards a game. Here you missed a punch, here you managed to hit your opponent and there you made a successful block. It's fun! It's interesting, exciting and challenging!" These words struck a chord with me and I will remember them forever.

Once I started to think about the fight as a game, I forgot about the pain but instead enjoyed the challenge. My parents found it difficult to believe, but after 2 months I even volunteered to participate in the Kyiv city karate championship.

The fight lasted a minute and a half. I punched, kicked and made blocks, but most often I was punched. After 45 seconds, I felt completely exhausted, like I couldn't even raise my hands, much less punch. The audience raved, "Andrii! Andrii! Kick his ass! Kill him!" When you hear your name cheered, it should give you more strength and power to win, but in my case it was the opposite. Guess what? My opponent's name was also Andrii! He had a green belt and more than 7 years of experience in karate.

I lost that fight. I was beaten up. But it was truly fun! Few things can compare to it.

After the fight, the trainer called me and said, "Andrii, you fought like a lion. I am proud of you. And by the way, you really challenged greatly this guy who won two previous city championships." Those were the nicest words that I ever heard. The next year I won many fights and even received a karate blue belt.

When you fight, winning or losing depends a lot on your attitude. If you are serious and think about how bad it will be if you lose, your subconscious will be blocked and won't give you great ideas about how to punch or block punches. Fighters who win are passionate about martial arts, have fun and consider a fight as a game.

According to researchers, over 98% of children younger than 10 years of age possess genius-level creativity. Children generate a lot of original ideas and they always have fun while generating them. When you have fun, you forget about time, you forget about mealtimes and activate your subconscious. It processes millions of thoughts at full capacity and eventually gives you amazing ideas in the form of a gut feeling, a hunch or intuition. There is a guaranteed way to not generate good ideas. Being serious! Unfortunately, seriousness is the state in which the majority of adults remain most of the time.

An environment of playfulness and humor is highly conducive to creativity. While you have fun, and your attitude towards the ideas generation process is as to a game, you are relaxed, excited, lively, open and confident. These are the characteristics of the high-performance state in which ideas are generated most effectively. Increase the amount of time you have fun in your life, do what you are passionate about and the amount of successful ideas that you generate will skyrocket. Whenever you are thinking hard about ideas and they are not coming, tell yourself, "Don't be so serious! Have fun! Generating ideas is an interesting and exciting game!"

Serious people have few ideas. People with ideas are never serious. – Paul Valery

Idea refinement

Idea evolution

Imagine that you were an inventor in the 14th century, went to the palace of the king and said, "Hurray, I invented a computer. Your Majesty, my new invention will allow you to browse the internet, read books, check emails and even watch movies." The king might say, "Are you nuts? We don't have electricity yet. Even though you are really smart, this invention is useless."

Motorola created the first handheld mobile phone. Apple created a mobile phone with a touch screen and millions of supported applications. Skype created an application that allows free video conversations through the internet. Motorola, Apple, Skype and thousands of other companies made enormous amounts of money just on the idea of the phone. Each idea evolves with time and to build a profitable business you need to make not more than one step in the evolution.

Don't try to create something unseen before and jump over many steps of evolution right away. Do sequential improvements. If you invented an electronic book reader device in the 14th century, your invention would be useless and ahead of its time. However, if you invented a printing press like Gutenberg, you would make a mark in history and make the world a better place.

Don't strive to be perfect, strive for continuous improvement

The biggest blocks to creativity are striving for perfection and fear of risk. Failures and imperfection are essential components of the successful idea generation process.

The initial ideas that you create often have flaws and require refinement before they are implemented. If you strive to create a perfect idea that will succeed guaranteed, you block your creativity and will only be able to reiterate old ideas that worked in the past.

When great writers write a book, they first write everything that comes to their mind on paper. Then this initial draft goes through many iterations of editing and becomes a great book. When you think about a question, your subconscious will rarely give you a fully refined answer; most often it is just a hint, an insight or a partial idea. Just like a writer edits his or her writing, you should improve your ideas before they become products, processes or actions. Don't strive to create perfect ideas, strive to create many ideas. They can always be improved later.

Modifying an existing product or service

The Transformer and SCAMPER techniques are proven to be invaluable for creating successful business ideas. These two techniques can help you generate a lot of great ideas necessary to create a profitable business, effective process or popular product.

Transformer

A Transformer technique is very simple but will allow you to create very successful businesses by challenging the status quo.

List rules and parameters of the business and then challenge them. Changing the rules may create an idea for a new successful business or a way to transform an existing one. Let's review how the Transformer technique can be applied in 3 examples below.

In a zoo animals live in cages and a zoo is open during the daytime. Let's challenge these rules. "Animals move freely around the zoo and it is open during nighttime." The Singapore zoo implemented this idea in a very popular attraction called Night Safari. Visitors travel in a tram across 7 geographical zones and observe nocturnal animals in their natural habitat. http://www.nightsafari.com.sg

A traditional circus features separate performances of acrobats, animals and clowns without a common theme. Guy

Laliberte challenged this assumption and said, "I will create a circus show with a common theme and with only acrobats." He created Cirque du Soleil which is a billion-dollar business and is extremely popular around the world. http://www.cirquedusoleil.com

Bands play music on real instruments such as a guitar, a piano or a violin. The band plays music and the audience listens. Recycled Percussion band challenged these assumptions. In addition to traditional instruments, the group uses buckets and recycled materials. Each audience member receives an instrument with a drumstick and actively participates in the performance. After watching Recycled Percussion in Las Vegas, my dad said it was the best show he has ever seen. http://www.recycledpercussionband.com

Just because things have always been done in a certain way in business doesn't mean they can't be done better or differently. Get in a habit of listing characteristics of a business or a process and thinking about how to challenge them. Using the Transformer technique, you will be able to transform your existing business or find an idea for a new successful business. The best idea creators constantly challenge status quo, assumptions, rules and beliefs. Always ask, "How can I break this rule? What if I challenge this belief?"

SCAMPER

Remember what ideas are created from? Ideas are modifications or combinations of other ideas. SCAMPER (Substitute, Combine, Adapt, Magnify or Minimize, Put to other use, Eliminate, Rearrange or Reverse) is a very popular creative technique, because of its effectiveness for generating high-quality business ideas. SCAMPER allows you to apply most common modifications to the product or process and create new business ideas. Imagine that you parked your car near a café. You entered into the building, the waiter brought a menu and you ordered a dinner. After the meal you asked for a bill and left a tip. Let's use the SCAMPER technique for this regular café to see which new business ideas we can generate.

Substitute. Let's substitute driving to the café to the café coming to your house. Do you see which business ideas we can create based on this substitution? Pizza delivery services use this exact business model. You call the phone number, order your meal and it is delivered to your house in less than an hour.

Combine. Let's combine a café and a thrill ride. For example, a result can be a Belgian Dinner in The Sky restaurant service which uses a crane to lift people, dinners and tables 150 feet into the air. Forbes magazine called it one of the world's ten most unusual restaurants.

Adapt. Let's adapt a café for kids. How might such a café look? All dishes have funny titles adapted for kids and are served with a toy. The café has a playground and waiters are dressed in costumes of characters from popular cartoons. When I was in New York for the first time, a tour guide showed a doll store. This store has a café where girls can drink tea with their dolls.

Magnify or minimize. Let's reduce the number of items on the menu to several drinks and sandwiches. As a result we may get a fast food restaurant such as McDonald's, Burger King or KFC.

Now let's reduce the number of dishes to just three. As a result we can get a business lunch combo that the café offers from noon until 3 p.m.

Put to other use. The building of the café can be used to create a hairdressing salon, a pharmacy or a shop. Dining tables can be used as office desks. The kitchen can produce cooked food that will be sold through supermarkets or sandwiches that will be sold through gas stations.

Eliminate. Let's eliminate a building of the café. As a result we may have a drive-in café where you order and eat food while sitting in a car. Let's eliminate the waiters and we can get a help-yourself café where you put food on your plate yourself and later pay for it at the counter.

Rearrange or reverse. Let's reverse a statement, "Visitors should leave tips for waiters" to "Visitors shouldn't leave tips." As a result we can have a café where waiters don't receive tips.

To be honest I hate paying tips. When I lived in Ann Arbor, Michigan, one day, while walking along the street, I stumbled upon a café with a sign on the door: "We don't take tips." I entered and placed an order. When the waitress arrived she said, "Here is your meal. And I just want to remind you that our café has a no tips policy." Should I tell you that I became a regular visitor?

SCAMPER and Transformer are thinking techniques that can bring you a lot of successful business ideas. Apply them occasionally to see if you can improve your existing business or start a new one. These techniques will help your subconscious see new opportunities quicker. Some of these opportunities will eventually turn into successful businesses.

Creativity in business is all about asking questions and thinking about answers. SCAMPER and Transformer help you to ask some of the good questions; your subconscious will generate ideas for you.

Mistakes lead to progress

Creativity is a probability game

One day there lived a young man called James who decided to open his own business. James thought, "I have an idea for a product that will change the world!" For 2 months James worked on developing his product and setting up the marketing campaign. Every morning he woke up with excitement, began working and finished only very late at night. This was the happiest time in James's life because he did what he loved and what he believed in. When the product was finally launched, James didn't sell anything and realized that nobody in the market wanted it. He thought, "I just don't have entrepreneurial talent! What did I hope for? I am not the business shark, just an ordinary James."

People tend to take it very personally when their ideas fail. The story about James is a story about millions of entrepreneurs worldwide. Some of them become very sad after the first couple of failures and stop trying new ideas, others realize that failures are an essential part of success and succeed.

Nature creates multiple species and lets a process of natural selection decide which will survive. Ninety-five percent of new species die and only the few strongest survive. Great idea creators know that just like in nature, to create a successful business you need to implement multiple ideas and let the market decide which of them will survive.

Research shows that successful artists, composers, scientists, writers and entrepreneurs not only succeed more often than others but also fail significantly more. They know that creativity is a probability game and the more ideas you implement, the more successful ones will be among them.

If you want to become good at business, make sure that your attitude towards failures is as follows: "Creativity is a probability game. I am excited to fail because the more I fail the more successful I become."

Failures are a valuable experience

One of the greatest scientists of the 20th century, Thomas Edison, created 10,000 prototypes before presenting to the world a commercially viable light bulb. He said, "I have not failed 10,000 times. I have not failed once. I have succeeded in proving that those 10,000 ways will not work. When I have eliminated the ways that will not work, I will find the way that will work."

The greatest innovators know that to become successful you need to make good decisions. Good decisions come from experience and experience comes from bad decisions. When you fail, you learn what doesn't work and why. This experience is the reason why you eventually succeed.

Everybody knows the Apple computer that Steve Jobs created, the light bulb that Edison invented and the theory of relativity that Einstein developed. Few people know that these great thinkers also implemented a large amount of ideas that didn't succeed. In creative thinking, quality comes from quantity and the more successful businesses you create the more failures you encounter along the way.

The best innovators fail often. The best innovators fail eagerly. The best innovators know that they are successful because they have failed more than others. The more ideas you generate and the more of them you implement, the sooner you will create something great. If you want to become a world-class ideas creator, expect that many of your ideas will fail, some will succeed and a few will have potential to change the world.

Become an accidental entrepreneur

One day in 1928 a Scottish biologist, Alexander Fleming, forgot to clean his laboratory before going on vacation. In 2 weeks, when Alexander returned from vacation, he saw that one of the staphylococcus culture plates in the corner of the laboratory was contaminated by a strange fungus, which prevented the growth of staphylococcus bacteria. After examination of the fungus, he noticed that it produced a substance that killed many disease-causing bacteria. This observation led Alexander to develop penicillin, an antibiotic that made one of the biggest breakthroughs in medicine and allowed the treatment of such dangerous illnesses as meningitis, gonorrhea and syphilis.

Penicillin, pacemakers, plastic, vulcanized rubber, Teflon, corn flakes, saccharin and numerous other inventions were made by accident. In business, successful ideas are often created by chance after a mistake, failure or coincidence, and your goal is to increase the probability of this chance many times.

Talk to as many people as you can, travel, experiment in business, read books, do different hobbies and try everything you haven't tried before. Coming up with a successful business idea by accident is the same as winning a lottery. Every life experience you have gives you an additional lottery ticket. The more active and versatile your life is, the higher are your chances to win a creative lottery and stumble upon a successful business idea.

Many people lose opportunities that life gives them, because they blindly follow their preconceived plan. Creative geniuses look forward to accidental discoveries and once they notice something interesting, drop everything they do to study it.

Appreciate all ideas that come to your head even if they are irrelevant to what you work on. Look forward to accidental discoveries and once you win the creative lottery, do everything to save, analyze and implement the successful business idea that came to your head. Be sure that some of these accidental ideas will have the same impact on your business as penicillin had on medicine.

Physical Fitness, Sleep and Energy

Good sleep and physical exercises not only help to maintain good health but also stimulate generation of business ideas.

Sleep

Many people think, "To become successful I need to do more work and stay awake longer. Time spent sleeping is time wasted." In fact, most productive thinkers sleep on average longer than other people.

The subconscious mind is responsible for generating successful business ideas and it works best when your conscious mind is inactive and especially well during sleep. If you need a good idea you are much more likely to generate it after 8 hours of healthy sleep than after a night of staring at the computer screen.

The best inventors are aware of the power of sleep and use it daily. In fact, they create a lot of breakthrough ideas during sleep or a nap. In terms of generating successful business ideas, sleep is certainly not a waste of time. In fact, it can be the most productive time of the day.

Physical exercises

Researchers found that regular physical exercises improve memory, mood and creative thinking. If you need to create good ideas or prepare for an exam, you will be more productive after jogging, swimming or taking a dancing class.

Physical exercises stimulate greatly the creative brain to think during the ideas incubation period. When you dance, run or swim, the conscious brain rests and the subconscious mind processes millions of thoughts. You might realize that the problem you have been thinking about the whole day is often solved either while you exercise or soon after.

The world's best thinkers know that if you need good ideas regularly, exercises are not optional because without them after a couple of weeks or months the creative productivity drops. Exercise at least two or three times per week and it will not only boost your energy but will also make you a better thinker.

You can't create anything awesome if you are not well rested or if you have low energy. Sleep well and exercise regularly. These two habits will not only keep you healthy but will also allow you to create a lot of excellent business ideas.

If you are stuck with a problem, go to sleep or exercise. Very likely the insight will come to you during the next thinking session.

Ideas-stimulating environment

Where to think best

Change the surroundings

One day, I was waiting for my wife on the bench in the hairdressing salon. I opened a notebook and began writing. The place was noisy and the bench uncomfortable but somehow my brain turned into an exceptionally creative mode and I wrote perhaps my best story ever.

For your brain it doesn't matter where to think; in a comfortable corner office, in a hairdressing salon or in a supermarket line. What is really important is that places where you think are occasionally changed. Our brain is stimulated by images that it sees. If you work in the same place every day and see the same images, eventually your creative brain will become lazy.

Your brain can be extremely productive in a hotel, in an airport lounge, in the back seat of a cab, in an office, at home, in a café or any other place, but under one condition. Locations where you think are occasionally changed. If your eyes see different surroundings during thinking sessions, your subconscious will be stimulated and will think at full capacity.

For an idea generation session, extract yourself from your everyday surroundings and go to a café, a library or a park. Thinking about ideas for 2 hours at an unusual location may bring you more ideas than a day of staring at the computer screen in the office. Don't think too hard about where to think, because any place that you don't visit regularly will stimulate your creative brain. If you asked me, "Andrii, where do you get your best ideas?" I would say, "In a hotel room, while taking a walk, in the shower, in a supermarket, during a boring meeting, when I jog at a stadium, in a cab, in the airport or while chatting with a friend in a café." The only thing that is common among places where our brains generate their best ideas is that they are different from where we spend most of our working time.

NeuroLeadership Institute's executive director, David Rock, surveyed over 6,000 people to discover where their best ideas were generated. Only 10% of respondents indicated that their best ideas came to them in the office, 39% said that their best ideas came to them at home and 51% said that their best ideas came to them neither at home nor at the office, but while traveling, jogging, eating in a café, at the park, in the swimming pool, at the beach, in a museum etc. This research confirms that the best ideas are generated when we get out of the surroundings that the brain sees the majority of the time.

In the office or at home

You can change scenery even without leaving an office. Simply changing pictures on the walls or moving from one desk to another may improve your creative thinking. Many companies that rely on creativity have many locations inside the office building where each employee can work.

When you work at home, occasionally change locations. Work in a bedroom, in a living room or in a kitchen. Sit on a sofa, at a desk or in an armchair. Changing locations inside your house can improve productivity of your thinking.

As a creative thinker, you should get used to changing scenery more often than other people. Travel whenever you can, work outside of your home or office whenever you can, utilize places where people kill time as your creative studio whenever you can. The more you change locations where you think, the more actively your brain will think and the more successful business ideas you will be able to produce. Change the rooms and locations in the rooms where you think to not let your brain become stale.

Go for a walk

Jean-Jacques Rousseau, the famous French philosopher, Johann Wolfgang von Goethe and Sigmund Freud created some of their best ideas while taking a walk. Taking a walk put them into creative mode and accelerated their thinking.

Walking is a monotonous physical activity that stimulates your subconscious mind and increases your chances to come up with a really good idea. When the landscape constantly changes in front of your eyes, the creative brain gets nurtured by fresh images and thinks more productively. If you are ever stuck and can't come up with good ideas, simply go for a walk. Great thinkers have been using a walk for centuries as a magic pill for stimulating their subconscious mind and getting into the creative state.

Any place is good

Think about ideas at places where most other people are just killing time: while walking to a parking lot, while waiting for a bus, while sitting at a boring meeting, at the airport or in the supermarket line. This habit will significantly improve the quality and quantity of ideas that you produce.

Some people think, "Creativity is a difficult and unpleasant job because I have to sit for hours and stare at the wall until a good idea comes." In fact, the best strategy is to think about ideas in the breaks between other activities and only for a few minutes. This approach will not only make generating ideas fun and easy but will also make your thinking more productive. Remember that you don't need an expensive chair or a fancy office for creating successful business ideas. Your creative studio is wherever you are at the particular moment. Innovative ideas often come in places that you least expect them.

Travel

Many great thinkers have created some of their best business ideas during their travel abroad.

A trip to Denmark inspired Walt Disney to create ideas that he later implemented in Disneyland. Walt wanted Disneyland to have a similar atmosphere of relaxed fun that the Tivoli Gardens amusement park in Copenhagen had.

During his vacation in Jamaica, Richard Branson listened to many local reggae bands. This trip inspired him to create a reggae record label and he signed contracts with over 20 reggae artists.

During his trip to Italy, Howard Schulz noticed that coffee bars existed almost everywhere and not only served excellent espresso, but also served as meeting places for people. Based on his memories of the cafés in Italy, he created Starbucks in the USA that not only served hot coffee but also provided customers with a great experience.

When you travel your brain gets exposed to an environment and experiences that are dramatically different from what you see daily. The dramatic change in surroundings serves as incredibly powerful stimulation for the brain. In fact, it is so powerful that many people say they become more creative not only for the duration of their travel but also for a few more weeks after they arrive home. Whenever you have an opportunity – travel, because travel is one of the most effective creative stimulators in the world.

To make your brain work at maximum capacity, don't let it get too accustomed to your everyday surroundings. Occasionally, change locations where you think: travel to other countries, change locations within a city, move around the office or house. This habit will help you avoid creative blocks and become more effective at producing excellent business ideas.

Mindless activities

Next time when you are bored...

Our brain is an incredibly powerful thinking machine, but when we are busy much of this capacity is unavailable. When we are bored and perform mindless activities, our analytical brain doesn't work and allows the subconscious mind to think at full capacity. Although washing dishes, ironing, jogging on a treadmill or staring at the wall in a subway car doesn't sound inspiring, these activities are very stimulating for creative thinking.

Next time you are bored or need to kill time, instead of listening to an MP3 player, playing games on a mobile phone or reading a book, give your brain a task to think about a particular problem and give your mind a chance to wander. By the time the mindless, repetitive or boring activity is over, you will have generated a lot of interesting ideas. When great thinkers are waiting in line, mowing the lawn or cleaning, they say, "Wow! It's boring. What a fruitful time to think about new ideas."

Idea shower

The executive director of the NeuroLeadership Institute in the U.S., David Rock, polled over 6,000 people to figure out where they generate their best ideas. Guess what? The shower was the most often mentioned location.

Although a shower doesn't look as inspirational as a hammock on the beach at the ocean, it is indeed an incredibly stimulating place for generating ideas. Firstly, a shower is a mindless activity that stimulates daydreaming. Secondly, warm water makes your body relaxed, which is important for high performance of the subconscious mind. Finally, when you go to the shower you change location, which stimulates the brain with a new experience.

Don't waste your shower time! Set tasks for the subconscious and after almost every trip to the shower you will come back with one, two or three good ideas. Make sure to write down all ideas, sometimes even before you finish washing yourself because ideas are the most fragile thing in the world and can evaporate as unexpectedly as they come.

Ideas breed ideas

Ideas stimulate ideas

While talking to an interesting person, listening to a presentation or reading an article, you can often come up with more interesting ideas than during the entire day of sitting at the desk and looking at the wall. Do you know why?

The answer to this question is one of the most important principles of creativity that says: "Ideas stimulate ideas." When you hear or read ideas of other people, they can trigger your brain and inspire you to generate another idea that is either relevant or irrelevant to the topic of the conversation, presentation or article. The more you expose your brain to ideas of other people, the more triggers will be pressed in your brain and the more interesting ideas you will generate.

Great thinkers know this powerful creativity principle and nurture their brains with huge quantities of ideas on a regular basis. They learn the ideas of others that are already successful, ideas that are in the implementation stage and ideas that have just been generated.

If you are working on a problem, expose yourself to external ideas as much as you can. All of them can trigger your brain and stimulate it to look at the problem in a fresh way and generate a successful solution. One of the most effective techniques for stimulating the brain is "ideas bombarding."

Ideas bombarding

This technique will allow you to effectively produce original ideas in a very short period of time. Within 2 hours, look through 100 ideas related to the same task and think about how they can be applied in your existing or future business. Think about how combinations or modifications of these ideas may help you to solve the same task most effectively.

For example, look through websites in your niche to see which ideas you can use on your website. Think about how you can modify these ideas to make them applicable for your business. If you are an author and want to create a title for your book – look through 100 book titles in your genre and see if they can inspire you to create an interesting title for your next book. Write down all the ideas that come to your head during this session.

New ideas are created on top of old ideas. Letting hundreds of ideas through your head will significantly stimulate your right brain to generate successful business ideas within a short period of time. "Ideas bombarding" is one of the most effective creative thinking techniques that exist and it will allow you to generate a lot of excellent ideas, some of which will make your business enormously successful.

Snowball effect

Ideas have a snowballing effect. Once you get any idea, no matter how crazy or unrealistic, further ideas will come faster to your head. As Cliff Einstein, the head of an advertising agency, said, "The best way to get an idea is to get an idea."

Once you think about a task or a problem, the first ideas will come to your head slowly. Then, ideas will come easier and eventually they will come so fast that it will be even difficult to record them. Don't stop this amazing flow of ideas by analyzing or criticizing them. Just appreciate what the subconscious does for you and quickly write down all thoughts and ideas that it generates. You will have plenty of opportunities to analyze and modify them later.

Value and respect all ideas that come to your head. The most crazy and unworkable idea may trigger something in your brain and allow you to come up with a great idea. Remember that there are no bad ideas. There are only successful ideas and ideas that lead us to successful ideas.

When people meet, magic happens

Conversation is a cradle of ideas

During the Age of Enlightenment (17th and 18th centuries) in England, more breakthroughs in art and science were made than during the previous thousand years. Interestingly enough, the beginning of the Age of Enlightenment coincides with the time when coffee was brought to England and coffee houses became popular around the country.

At the beginning of the 17th century, water wasn't safe to drink in England and people had to drink beer or wine for breakfast, lunch and dinner. As you can imagine, the cafés at that time were full of drunk people and weren't suitable for intellectual conversations. After coffee and tea became popular, coffee houses became a place where scientists, artists and great thinkers met and exchanged ideas. These casual conversations often led to breakthroughs in science, literature and art.

Many great ideas are born during your conversation with another person. When your thinking mate hears your raw idea, he or she may share an opinion, hint or thought that can help to make it better. After several rounds of thoughts exchange, your raw idea will evolve, get shaped and become a valuable idea ready for implementation.

Often our subconscious mind generates seeds for the good ideas. Conversation is a soil that allows these seeds to grow into accomplished, high-quality ideas ready for implementation. Many significant advances in business, art and science were made during a casual conversation. Great thinkers often share ideas with other people, because they know that the thoughts exchange significantly improves their creative output.

Innovation comes from people meeting up in the hallways or calling each other at 10:30 at night with a new idea, or because they realized something that shoots holes in how we've been thinking about a problem.
– Steve Jobs

Engage other people to give you ideas

Last year, I launched a contest for the cover design of my book *Magic of Impromptu Speaking* and during the first round received 104 designs from 23 contestants. I showed the top 5 designs to my wife and together we agreed that one of the concepts was significantly stronger than the others. Olena pointed at this design and said, "This cover is great, but it would become stronger with a different background color and slightly changed fonts." I thought that what Olena said made sense and requested a designer to send me several versions of the same cover, however with changes that my wife suggested. One of the covers the designer sent in response became the cover with which the book got published. Many readers sent me emails saying that the cover of *Magic of Impromptu Speaking* is one of the best book covers they have ever seen. Do the readers care that 25 people in total were engaged in developing an idea for the book cover design? No, the only thing they care about is that the cover looks compelling.

You significantly limit your creative potential if you think that all good ideas should be generated, modified and improved only by your own brain. Talk about your problem with other people and use their thoughts, hints and suggestions extensively.

If I didn't engage 24 other people in creating an idea for the *Magic of Impromptu Speaking* book cover, I would not have such a successful design. It's OK that not all of the excellent thoughts popped up in your head, what matters is the end result. Engage as many people in thinking about your tasks as you need and they will increase the quality of your business ideas.

Filtering and executing ideas

3 categories technique

When you have generated and analyzed a significant amount of ideas, you need to select the most promising among them, and the most effective strategy to do so is to use the approach that judges use during castings of the American TV show *So You Think You Can Dance*. If a person danced really well, judges say, "You get a ticket to Las Vegas for the second stage of the selection process." If judges are on the fence, they say, "We invite you to the short test in the afternoon, to see how you can pick up professional choreography." If the dance was clearly bad, the judges say, "You are not ready for this show." This selection process allows judges to select the best dancers out of thousands of candidates within a short period of time.

Imagine that each idea on your list is a candidate and you are a judge. Once you see that an idea is clearly good, mark it with "great idea," if the idea is clearly bad, mark it with "won't fly," and if you are on the fence, mark it with "interesting."

Use your gut feeling and common sense to decide in which category to put each idea. If, for example, you want to introduce a new product to the market, put yourself in your customers' shoes and ask, "Would I buy it?" If you like the product yourself, chances are that many other people will like it, too.

Cross out ideas that "won't fly." Save "interesting ideas" for the future. After further examination and modification you may decide to move them into the "great ideas" category. Move "great ideas" to the next round of the selection process.

Creative buddy

Your creative buddy is the first person with whom you share ideas. A creative buddy can highlight the potential problems in ideas that you haven't noticed as well as suggest how to improve them. Find a person with whom you are on the same wavelength, whom you enjoy being around and whose opinion you trust.

For example when I generate ideas, I first share them with my wife. I know that Olena honestly says if she thinks the idea is good or not and her opinion is always valuable. Time has proven that if Olena approved an idea, the probability that it will become successful is higher.

Your creative buddy can be your better half, friend, colleague or business partner, but most important is that you have an easy rapport with this person and are not afraid to share your silliest ideas. Most people won't be honest with their criticism, but the creative buddy will. Most people won't give you an opinion that you trust, but the creative buddy will. The world's best thinkers know the importance of having a creative buddy and spend years developing relationships with people who they can trust. After your creative buddy has told you that the idea is good, it's worth exposing it to a larger group of people.

Use the opinions of others as additional information for consideration but make a final decision regarding the idea yourself. Remember that there are numerous examples in history where nobody besides the idea creator believed in the idea but eventually it became extraordinarily successful. Once you have made your own analysis and received external opinions, implement your best ideas and let the market say which of them are viable.

Implement ideas with little risk

Take it for granted that no matter how much you analyze an idea and how much feedback you get, it is impossible to predict with 100% probability if it will become successful. Billions of dollars are lost every year by companies who invest in ideas that sound great on paper but, once faced with the real world, fail due to various reasons.

Great thinkers know, "Only the market can make the final decision of whether the idea is viable. The best way to see if an idea is worth significant investment of time and money is to implement it with little risk."

Imagine that you own an international chain of restaurants and want to introduce a new snack to the menu. Introduce it first in a single restaurant or a single city. If the snack proves to be popular, invest in introducing it on a larger scale; if not, you haven't lost a lot of time and money. By testing your ideas before implementing them on a large scale, you minimize the losses in case of failure.

At the international design firm IDEO the employees do frequent and quick prototyping for product ideas. At Pixar, animators show their work in early stages to the entire animation crew. Test your ideas on a small scale and let unsuccessful ones fail as soon as possible to minimize your expenses and time loss. If the idea doesn't fail at the test stage, invest more money and time into it because, most likely, it is one of those ideas that will make your company highly successful.

Implement your best ideas with a small investment of time and money and let the market decide which of them will survive. Immediately discard ideas that failed during the test stage and invest in those that worked. This strategy will allow you to build a profitable business with minimum risk.

Failures are an essential part of the creative process and the greater the number of your ideas that fail, the more will eventually succeed. The world's most successful thinkers have more failures than other people but they are small and affordable.

"100, 20, 5, 1" rule

Once you have generated hundreds of ideas you may ask, "How can I figure out which of them will become successful?" The "100, 20, 5, 1" rule says that after going through the list of 100 ideas, you reduce it to the 20 most promising ones on your own. After asking for the opinion of your creative buddy and the small group of potential customers, you further reduce the list to 5 ideas worth implementing. After implementing 5 ideas, 4 of them either fail or give mediocre results but 1 becomes incredibly successful. Of course 100, 20, 5, 1 are only ballpark figures, but they give a good estimate of what it takes to get one idea that will make a significant positive impact on your business. Some of the greatest ideas in business history were selected using the "100, 20, 5, 1" rule.

Endure opposition and frustrations

Great ideas face opposition

When we create great ideas we expect people to say, "Wow! What a great idea! I can't wait to buy your products and services." However, very often even the most successful business projects in the world such as the telephone, radio and The Beatles band initially receive negative feedback and face opposition.

Associates of David Sarnoff replied to his request to invest in radio in 1921: "The wireless music box has no imaginable commercial value. Who would pay for a message sent to no one in particular?"

After the audition by The Beatles, the Decca Records executive gave his verdict to the band's manager: "Not to mince words, Mr. Epstein, but we don't like your boys' sound. Groups are out; four-piece groups with guitars particularly are finished."

Western Union officials who reviewed Alexander Graham Bell's offer to purchase his telephone patent wrote: "The Telephone purports to transmit the speaking voice over telegraph wires. We found that the voice is very weak and indistinct, and grows even weaker when long wires are used between the transmitter and receiver. Technically, we do not see that this device will ever be capable of sending recognizable speech over a distance of several miles. Messer Hubbard and Bell want to install one of their 'telephone devices' in every city. The idea is idiotic on the face of it. Furthermore, why would any person want to use this ungainly and impractical device when he can send a messenger to the telegraph office and have a clear written message sent to any large city in the United States?"

You might ask, "Why does it happen?" Well, there are 3 major reasons why people say "It won't work" even to the world's greatest ideas:

Firstly, people are often averse to the unknown and, just like David Sarnoff's associates, don't realize the potential of the product before they have seen, tested or used it. Once you have implemented an idea and received positive feedback from your first customers, the same people will say that your idea is great.

Secondly, many people are too concentrated on their past experience and make predictions about the future based on what worked in the past. For example, the Decca Records executive knew many four-piece bands that were not popular and after seeing that The Beatles band consisted of four musicians made a prediction that it would fail.

Finally, many people tend to concentrate on why the idea won't work rather than how to make it work or what potential it may have. Just like with the idea of the telephone, it is possible to find plenty of reasons "Why it won't work" for almost any idea. That's why even most successful ideas in the world initially faced opposition.

Use feedback from people you share ideas with as additional information for consideration but remember that even the world's best ideas initially faced opposition. If you believe in an idea, implement it no matter what everyone else is saying so you don't regret your entire life that you didn't.

It's really hard to design products by focus groups. A lot of times, people don't know what they want until you show it to them. – Steve Jobs

If you have a good idea, 99 percent of people will tell you why it's not good or how it's been done before or why else you're going to fall flat on your face. You've just got to say, "Screw it, just do it" and get on with it. – Richard Branson

It's very difficult for people when they're doing their own thing to do it their own way entirely, not taking notes from anyone else, not taking anyone else's advice. Do it the way you want to do it, don't listen to other people. – James Dyson

Be persistent. Creative thinking is a marathon

In 1979 James Dyson bought one of the most advanced vacuum cleaners on the market, and after using it got frustrated with how quickly it clogged and began losing suction. James got excited about this problem and decided, "I will design a vacuum cleaner that will clean the house more effectively."

Partly supported by the salary of his wife, who worked as an art teacher, and partly by bank loans, James spent almost 5 years working on his vacuum cleaner design and after 5,126 failed prototypes eventually created a working version of a dual-cyclone bagless vacuum cleaner.

James realized that no company in the UK wanted to buy his technology or collaborate in manufacturing his vacuum cleaner, and retailers were reluctant to sell the product of an unknown brand. After generating many more interesting business ideas about how to overcome these obstacles, James first launched his vacuum cleaner through catalogue sales in Japan where it became incredibly successful. In a few years, the Dyson vacuum cleaner became one of the most desirable household appliances worldwide and James Dyson became a billionaire.

In an interview with Forbes magazine, James was asked if he ever wanted to give up. And here is what he replied: "I wanted to give up almost every day. But one of the things I did when I was young was long distance running, from a mile up to ten miles. They wouldn't let me run more than ten miles at school – in those days they thought you'd drop down dead or something. And I was quite good at it, not because I was physically good, but because I had more determination. I learned determination from it.

"More particularly, I learned that the moment you want to slow down is the moment you should accelerate. In long distance running, you go through a pain barrier. The same thing happens in research and development projects, or in starting any business. There's a terrible moment when failure is staring you in the face. And actually if you persevere a bit longer you'll start to climb out of it."

Of course in the majority of cases great thinkers don't encounter as many failures and difficulties as James Dyson did but they are all creative "long distance" runners. If you say to yourself, "I am in business for a long time, I am ready to endure frustrations and persist in creating and testing ideas on the way to achieving my dream," you are destined to have enormous success.

Success is a lousy teacher. It seduces smart people into thinking they can't lose. – Bill Gates

Creativity habit

Train creative muscles

In 7th grade, my math teacher Alexander said to my mother, "Victoria, your son's performance is very poor. Honestly, I think math isn't his thing. It would be better for Andrii if you transfer him to another school at the end of the year." My classmate Peter was a naturally gifted student and several heads above everyone I knew at math. He always solved problems nobody else could and Alexander called him "math heavy artillery."

In 8th grade, after one incident in class I became very interested in math. I began devoting all my spare time to math and by the end of the year became the second-best math student in the class after Peter. In 9th grade, Peter became very interested in guitar, founded his own band and neglected math. By the end of the 9th grade, I outperformed Peter and became the strongest math student in the entire school. In 10th grade, I continued devoting at least 4 hours a day to solving problems and by the end of the year became one of the 100 best math students in the Ukraine.

Peter is certainly much more gifted than I am, but I trained significantly more. I am sure that if he devoted at least half the time that I did to math he would achieve far better results than I. If you are interested to know what happened to Peter later, he became a guitar player in one of the most popular bands in the Ukraine.

When a person finishes a marathon in under 3 hours we don't say, "Wow, he is a running genius," we say, "He or she trained a lot. Anybody can run a marathon in under 3 hours after a couple of years of daily training."

However, when talking about the world's best thinkers, people often say, "They are geniuses. I will never be able to create such awesome ideas." Guess what? The world's best thinkers are able to generate successful ideas not because they are geniuses, but because they think about ideas daily and have trained their creative muscles more than other people. If you practice generating ideas regularly, after some time you will produce better ideas than the majority of naturally gifted people, because your creative muscles will be stronger.

Any person who trained for a marathon for several years would outperform a gifted runner who didn't. Any person who practices creativity daily will outperform at creating successful business ideas any genius who doesn't.

The more you practice pushups, the more pushups you will be able to do. The same happens with ideas. The more you practice creative thinking, the quicker high-quality ideas will come to your head. If you take practicing ideas generation seriously, in a few years other people may call you a creative genius.

The majority of people rarely give tasks to their subconscious and once they see that their creative muscles are weak say, "I am just not a creative type." It sounds the same as, "I exercise only twice a year and can't do more than 5 pushups. I don't have the talent for pushups."

Fortune top-15 writers write about 5 novels a year. How can they be that productive? They write daily and their writing muscles are very strong. If you want to become world-class at generating business ideas, you need to exercise your creative muscles regularly. If you think about ideas daily, you will generate better ideas than naturally gifted people who don't.

Certainly, every child is born blessed with a vivid imagination. But just as muscles grow flabby with disuse, so the bright imagination of a child pales in later years if he ceases to exercise it. – Walt Disney

Develop a creativity habit

Anders Ericsson studied young violinists and pianists in their early twenties at the Music Academy of West Berlin. He asked music professors to split students into 3 groups: exceptional students most likely to become international solo performers, very good students most likely to join the world's best orchestras and least able students most likely to become music teachers.

Ericsson discovered that students in all groups had remarkably similar backgrounds and the only difference between them was the amount of practice time. By the age of 20, exceptional students had practiced on average 10,000 hours; good pianists and violinists 8,000 hours and those most likely to become music teachers 4,000 hours.

Everybody who was in the elite group of top musicians had spent on average 10,000 hours practicing during their lifetime and everybody who had spent at least 10,000 hours practicing was in the elite group of top musicians. Further research of top chess players, dancers, salespeople and scientists confirmed that the amount of practice rather than talent makes a person an expert in his or her domain. Ericsson wrote, "The differences between expert performers and normal adults reflect a life-long persistence of deliberate effort to improve performance."

The same is true in creativity. The more experience you have in creating ideas, the faster your brain will make connections and generate successful business ideas. To become an exceptional thinker you need to develop a habit of thinking about ideas daily.

Practicing ideas generation is easier than playing chess, violin or piano because the majority of thinking is done by the creative brain while you are not consciously thinking. However, to activate your creative brain you need to think about ideas that can improve your life regularly for at least 15 minutes.

The more you practice thinking creatively, the less time it will take to come up with a great business idea and the more you will enjoy the process. After some time you will become a world-class thinker and exceptional ideas will come to your head in abundance.

Final checklist

To significantly increase the quantity and quality of ideas that you generate, reading this book isn't enough. You need to make principles from this book a part of your own habits.

Below you will find the 7 most fundamental principles of creating successful business ideas. Write them down on a sheet of paper and hang it near the desk where you work or near your bed. Over the next 3 weeks, think for at least 15-30 minutes per day about ideas using these principles. These can be ideas that will help you improve your business, achieve your dreams or make your life more interesting. I promise you that by the end of these 3 weeks you will notice a significant jump in your creative performance.

1. **Collect raw materials.** Ideas are combinations or modifications of other ideas. The more you know the ideas of other people and the more life experiences you expose yourself to, the more creative raw materials you have. The more creative raw materials you have, the more combinations your subconscious mind will be able to make and the more likely you are to create new valuable and interesting ideas.

2. **Set the task for the subconscious mind.** Your subconscious mind is a powerful thinking mechanism, but it remains idle if you haven't given it a task. Once you begin giving your subconscious questions to think about regularly, you will notice how the quantity and quality of your ideas will skyrocket.

3. **Separate analyzing and generating ideas.** When you are analyzing ideas, your analytical brain blocks your superfast creative brain from thinking. To let the creative brain do its work, separate the processes of analyzing and generating ideas.

4. **Think and rest.** The most effective thinking algorithm is the following: think about a problem for an extensive period of time, forget about the problem and rest, occasionally think about the problem for few minutes and forget about it again. The incubation period when you don't think about the problem is essential for your subconscious mind to process millions of thoughts and combinations of ideas, however to give it a task you need to think for some time about the problem consciously.

5. **Generate many ideas.** In creative thinking, quantity equals quality. You can't generate one great idea. However, you can generate many ideas and select one or several great ideas out of them.

6. **Have fun.** Your subconscious mind thinks most effectively when you have fun. When you are serious, you are very unlikely to create really creative and valuable ideas.

7. **Believe and desire.** Believe that you will generate great ideas and have a burning desire to generate them. If you do, great ideas will come to you in abundance and sooner or later the problem will be solved.

Once you have made these 7 principles a part of your own creative habits, glance through the book again and practice other principles and techniques. In a year's time of practicing generating ideas regularly, you will become a world-class creative thinker. The skill of creating ideas will make your business successful and your life an adventure. I wish you good luck in creating successful ideas and in achieving all your dreams in business.

The Idea Lifestyle Bundle

The Idea Lifestyle Bundle

Magic of Impromptu Speaking

Create a Speech That Will Be Remembered for Years in Under 30 Seconds

Andrii Sedniev

The Idea Lifestyle Bundle

Why learn impromptu speaking?

Every day you speak with relatives, friends and strangers without needing preparation. Talking off the cuff, one on one is easy for most of us. When the quality of an impromptu speech is crucial, however, giving it becomes a huge problem.

How did you feel when you were asked to give an impromptu speech for the first time? I remember my grandma's birthday celebration 20 years ago, where my mom said, "Andrii, the next toast will be yours."

"Mom, please no! I don't know what to say."

"I am not going to discuss it with you, Andrii. You are next!"

I thought, "Oh, my god! The time passes so quickly! I will have to talk in just two minutes and I have no idea what to say! Everybody will see my embarrassment and I will feel so miserable."

Imagine that you are giving an interview live on CNN or answering a CEO's question in a boardroom. When the pressure is on for a high-quality speech, most speakers' minds go blank.

One answer during the job interview may determine whether you get the job of your dreams or not. One answer during the Q&A session may determine how potential customers perceive your competence. One answer during the TV debates may determine whether you become the president or not.

No matter what you do, you will encounter situations where you need to speak impromptu, and success in life may be determined by your impromptu speaking skills. Great impromptu speakers are extremely successful during TV interviews, Q&A sessions, networking events and even prepared speeches. Audiences love speakers who can go off script and improvise on stage. Those who can speak well off the cuff are better communicators, are more creative and have more interesting and versatile lives.

The good news is that you can become an outstanding impromptu speaker very quickly if you follow the right process.

What is Magic of Impromptu Speaking?

During the last 10 years, I collected tips, techniques and strategies that can dramatically raise the level of any speaker in impromptu speaking. My goal was to create the most comprehensive system, which will make anyone a world-class impromptu speaker within a very short time. The *Magic of Impromptu Speaking* system was based on the analysis of thousands of impromptu speaking contests, interviews, debates and Q&A sessions.

The results were astonishing. *Magic of Impromptu Speaking* students reported that not only did their ability to speak off the cuff improve significantly over a period of 2 months, but their lives also changed for the better.

Those who speak well impromptu, on average, get promotions faster, are more interesting to be around and are more creative in everyday life.

The system described in this book covers the most effective techniques not only from the world of impromptu speaking, but also from acting, stand-up comedy, applied psychology and creative thinking.

Once you master the system, you will grow immensely as an impromptu speaker. Your audience members will think that what you do on stage, after such short preparation, is pure magic and will recall some of your speeches many years later.

After you master all of the magic components of the *Magic of Impromptu Speaking* system, your audiences will look forward to hearing you again and again during Q&A sessions, interviews, wedding receptions or contests.

Magic of Impromptu Speaking did wonders for me, it did wonders for everybody who learned it, and it will do wonders for you. Are you ready to begin a journey into the magic world of impromptu speaking? Let's go!

Best improvisation isn't improvisation

Imagine that you participate in a public speaking workshop. During the Q&A section, you ask the trainer, "John, can you please tell …?" And John answers with humor, interesting stories and great delivery techniques. The audience applauds. You think, "Wow. John is obviously an amazing impromptu speaker. I would never be able to answer a question off the cuff so well."

You might not know that John has conducted this workshop hundreds of times and answered your question more than once before. He tried different versions of the answer, analyzed various audience reactions and eventually chose the answer that got the best audience response.

Imagine that in the afternoon you turn on the TV and see a politician answering questions on a show. He sounds very smooth, confident and eloquent. You may think, "Wow, this politician really knows what he is talking about. He has a gift for speaking impromptu. I wish I could speak like he does."

You might not know, though, that the interview questions were sent in advance and that the politician has not only rehearsed and practiced the answers, but also rejected some of the questions.

Imagine that on Sunday night you go to see an improv show with your family. At the beginning of the show, one of the actors tells the audience, "Please shout out a random word. We will use it later in our performance." After getting the words, the improv actors sing a song or create funny sketches. You laugh through the entire evening and say, "These guys are so talented. I can't believe they just did that amazing show without any preparation."

What you might not know is that the group has practiced the same sketch with different words numerous times. Parts of the song and parts of the sketch are well rehearsed. Also, some people in the audience are friends of the actors and the words they shout are predetermined.

Does knowing this information make the improv show less exciting for you? No. Does the answer of the politician seem less professional? No. Does John the trainer sound less interesting? Of course not.

No matter how well you can think on your feet, a completely improvised answer can rarely be better than a prepared one. To get ready for impromptu speaking competitions, the contestants prepare and rehearse short blocks of the speech and stories that they can use in response to many different questions. Once they go on stage, they partially speak off the cuff and partially use the rehearsed blocks. The audience laughs, applauds and enjoys the speech. Everybody sees the end result. Few people know how the impressive impromptu speech is prepared.

Certainly, there are great shows, interviews and Q&A answers that are done completely off the cuff, but the best are always prepared, at least partially. To become a great impromptu speaker you need to learn how to eliminate the impromptu factor as much as possible.

Think about what questions may be asked during the Q&A section

While you prepare your speech at home, think about what questions the audience may ask. In most cases, you will be able to guess the questions and prepare the answers in advance. If you are giving the same speech many times, the questions from your audience members repeat themselves. Think about how you can answer each particular question you have heard before during the next Q&A section.

Discuss the interview questions in advance

If you are participating in a TV show or an interview, ask for questions that you will be asked so that your answers can be prepared in advance.

If you participate in a job interview, research common interview questions for candidates that are posted on the internet. Very often, they are shared on specialized forums and discussion boards by former job candidates who interviewed with the same company.

If you are invited to a birthday or a wedding

If you are invited to a birthday party or a wedding reception, you may be asked to give a toast. The best toasts are personal, so think of something specific about the person who has a birthday or is getting married and how you can personalize the toast.

Develop your impromptu speaking skills

The number of completely different questions that you can be asked is limited. After enough practice, it will be difictul for any question to surprise you. You will think, "Ah, I have been asked a similar question before, I'd answer it this way …"

Many of the techniques you will learn later in Magic of Impromptu Speaking system will make you very effective at thinking on your feet. However, to make your improvisation on stage even more powerful, eliminate the impromptu factor as much as you can. The greatest impromptu speakers know that the best improvisation isn't improvisation.

The biggest secret of impromptu speaking

When I was about 12 years old, I had a huge fear. I was afraid of being beaten up by bullies in the street. I was so scared to go to school every day that my parents put me into the Kiokushin Karate school to get this fear out of me.

Every training session, after stretching and practicing punches, we had practice fights. I was fighting against, older, bigger and more experienced guys. It was painful, unpleasant and that time lasted an eternity for me.

One day our trainer, Alexander, said, "Please all sit in a circle. I have to tell you something." What he said not only changed my attitude to karate and fighting but also my attitude to impromptu speaking.

"Guys, don't fear the pain from the punches. Have an attitude to a fight as you would to a game. Here you missed a punch, here you managed to hit your opponent and there you made a successful block. It's fun! It's interesting, exciting and challenging!" These words struck a chord with me and I will remember them forever.

Once I started to think about the fight as a game, I forgot about the pain but instead enjoyed the challenge. My parents found it difficult to believe, but after 2 months I even volunteered to participate in the Kyiv city karate championship.

The fight lasted a minute and a half. I punched, kicked and made blocks, but most often I was punched. After 45 seconds, I felt completely exhausted, like I couldn't even raise my hands, much less punch. The audience raved, "Andrii! Andrii! Kick his ass! Kill him!" When you hear your name cheered, it should give you more strength and power to win, but in my case it was the opposite. Guess what? My opponent's name was also Andrii! He had a green belt and more than 7 years of experience in karate.

I lost that fight. I was beaten up. But it was truly fun! Few things can compare to it.

After the fight, the trainer called me and said, "Andrii, you fought like a lion. I am proud of you. And by the way, you really challenged greatly this guy who won two previous city championships." Those were the nicest words that I ever heard.

Was it painful to fight with the best karate fighter in Kyiv in full strength? Of course! Did I have bruises on my body after the fight? In fact, I had them almost everywhere. Was it fun? It was incredibly cool and this fight is one of my best childhood memories.

This karate championship had a tremendous effect on my development as a fighter, not only when sparring, but also in life. If you fight, your success is fully determined by your attitude. In impromptu speaking, it's the same. Your attitude fully determines your learning curve and success.

If you asked me, "Andrii, what is the most important technique to remember to become a world-class impromptu speaker?" I would say for sure, "Think about the impromptu speech as a game. Your attitude will change your frame of mind and instead of concentrating on the difficulty of finding the right words, your brain will deliver the perfect answer."

RELOCAte to a high-performance state

One day, while a student at the University of Michigan, I went to a bar with my friends and several alumni to celebrate the end of the school year. After we ordered drinks and started a conversation, I said something funny and everybody laughed. I told another joke and everybody laughed again. That afternoon the best comedians would have envied my ability to tell jokes on the spot, and for about 2 hours everyone was laughing really hard.

I often struggle to come up with a great joke, but that afternoon I couldn't stop the flow of amazing jokes coming to my mind.

Do you remember a time when you were much more effective than usual? The ideas were generated, the work was done quickly, your jokes were funny, and your impromptu speeches were great. This is a high-performance state. You have been in this state many times before and every time it felt like you were a rock star. What if you could be in this state during your next impromptu speech?

I have good news. You can get into a high-performance state quickly and whenever you want. The easiest way to get into this state is to use the RELOCAte technique developed by scientists who model and replicate behavior of successful people.

The research showed that in a high-performance state, people are relaxed, excited, lively, open and confident. The opposite is also true. If you become relaxed, excited, lively, open and confident simultaneously, you will get into the high-performance state and become dramatically more effective.

When actors play a role and want to convey a particular emotion of the character, they need to evoke it in themselves. They remember a situation from life when they felt this emotion clearly, relive it in their imagination and very soon begin to feel the emotion. This technique from the world of acting will help you with getting into the high-performance state.

To get into a high-performance state, you need to become simultaneously relaxed, excited, lively, open and confident. When these 5 states are combined, their individual effects on performance increase many times.

Relaxed

Relax all the muscles in your body completely except for the ones you need to stay upright. First, flex all your muscles and then quickly relax them. Relax all the muscles from your head to your feet. Pay attention to your breathing. Notice that each time you breathe and exhale, your body relaxes more and more until you are fully relaxed.

Excited

Remember a time in your life when you were really excited and relive this situation in your mind. Feel the excitement again. You are spontaneous and open for new opportunities and behaviors. Feel yourself excited and secure because your impromptu speech is just a game.

Lively

Become energetic. Feel the power within you and your readiness to do something. To become energetic, jump, dance, do physical exercise or just remember how it felt when you did something active. If you imagine it clearly enough, your nervous system won't notice any difference. Remember, however, that you need to build up your energy while staying completely relaxed. As soon as you notice tension – relax yourself. It might seem impossible to be lively and relaxed simultaneously, but it is easy. It's an amazing feeling of outside calmness and internal readiness.

Open

Remember a time when you were ready to accept anything that the world has to offer. You don't know what will happen in the next moment, but it is not important because you are ready to accept anything. Build up a feeling of openness until you can clearly feel it.

Confident

Recall a situation from your life when you felt absolutely confident in yourself. Maybe you said or did something you were 100% sure about. Relive it as clearly as you can and feel what you felt at that time. While building up a feeling of confidence, remain open, lively, excited and relaxed.

Again

Repeat again everything mentioned above! Every time you increase the intensity of each feeling, make sure you stay simultaneously relaxed, excited, lively, open and confident.

Go through this list several times and very soon you will get into a high-productivity state.

The high-productivity state will help you think quickly on your feet and create true impromptu magic on stage. I highly recommend getting into this state even when you give a prepared speech. It will allow you to be in the moment. It will allow you to improvise and make your speech special for your audience. RELOCAte is a very powerful technique that can get your impromptu speaking to the next level.

How to think on your feet

Stop internal dialogue

Numerous researches were conducted to compare the performance of our right brain (subconscious mind) and left brain (conscious mind). The results confirmed that our creative right brain is at least 2 million times faster than our analytical left brain.

Before you give an impromptu speech, there is usually very little time for preparation. As you can imagine, you need to think really fast. If you have less than 30 seconds to prepare an answer to a question, would you rather rely on your slow brain or your super-fast one?

If you want to become a world-class impromptu speaker and create speeches on the spot that will be remembered for years, your only choice is to use the creative super-fast brain as much as possible.

When an inexperienced impromptu speaker hears a question, he usually begins an internal dialogue, "Oh, I don't know what to say. No ... this won't be a perfect answer. What will everybody think about me? The time is passing so quickly and I still don't have any idea! Everybody will see my embarrassment and I will feel miserable."

When you speak to yourself, the internal dialogue blocks the super-fast creative brain and activates the analytical one. With such performance, it's impossible to think quickly and give a good answer.

To let your right brain and subconscious mind do their work, get rid of the internal dialogue. Don't let negative thoughts block your super-fast thinking. Once your brain is freed from the internal dialogue, it will process millions of options in a matter of seconds and will suggest the best possible answer to you. Just like anybody else, world-class speakers have the internal dialogue before the speech. The only difference is that they know exactly how to block it.

You may ask, "Andrii, how can I block the negative thoughts from popping up in my head and blocking my super-fast brain?"

To achieve this, you simply need to accept two beliefs of the world-class impromptu speaker: "I will definitely answer a question" and "I will not always have a stellar answer."

Once you make these two beliefs yours, nothing will stop your super-fast brain from creating a perfect answer. Without an internal dialogue, you will grow immensely as an impromptu speaker and the quality of your speeches will be apparent.

Beliefs of the world-class impromptu speaker

I will definitely answer a question

Imagine that you are a boxer and when a fight begins, a thought pops up in your mind: "I don't have a clue how to begin a fight. What if everybody doesn't like my punches?"

These thoughts not only will block your instincts and super-fast brain, but also will bring you pain from the opponent's punch.

When you are in a ring, there is no time for internal dialogue and self-analysis. You first get into the fight and only then decide what to do with your body. You don't know whether you will win. You don't know exactly how you will block and punch. The only thing you know for sure is that you will definitely fight and your instincts will tell you what to do at each particular moment.

The moment you think, "My opponent looks scary," "I don't want to be beaten up really hard" or "What if he is stronger than I thought?" – you have already lost. The professional fighters know that and their belief is, "I first get into the fight and only then decide what to do with my body. My instincts and years of training will help me to decide what to do at each particular moment."

The same principle applies to impromptu public speaking. The most important attribute for any impromptu speaker is a "can-do" state of mind. Your subconscious mind will give you a perfect answer. However, to let it work you need to block all the negative thoughts first. Forget about thoughts like "I am unprepared" or "I am afraid" because no matter whether you know what to say or not, you will begin speaking.

The belief of the greatest impromptu speakers is the following: "Whether I have good ideas or not I will give an answer. My experience speaking impromptu and the techniques I learned in the past will help me to figure out the best answer to a question."

Once you stop considering whether to give an answer or not and what the consequences might be, the quality of your speeches will increase dramatically. All of your brainpower will be focused on figuring out an answer instead of judging your answer or deciding whether to speak or not. The question is not whether you will answer the question. The question is how you will answer it.

Later in this book, you will learn how to give an answer even if you didn't come up with a good idea. But for now, remember! You always answer the question and never block your super-fast creative brain with internal dialogue.

I won't always give a stellar answer

If you are Michael Jordan, you don't always score the basket, you just do it more often than other players. Just admit it. You will not always have a stellar impromptu answer no matter how well trained you are.

Depending on the question and situation, the quality of your answer will be different. Your worthiest answers may be better than the best answers of untrained speakers, but you need to accept the fact that not all your impromptu speeches will be stellar.

Everyone wants to give outstanding responses and receive standing ovations, but it just doesn't happen every time in impromptu speaking.

If you are worried about the quality of your answer, you begin thinking about the potential consequences of a poor answer. Self-analysis blocks your super-fast brain and leads to a guaranteed weak answer.

Just as Michael Jordan tries his best to make a shot, try to respond to the question the best you can. Don't worry about the quality of your answers. The sooner you accept the fact that not all your questions will be stellar, the sooner you will join the ranks of the world's best impromptu speakers.

Remember that impromptu speaking is just a game. No matter which answer you give, it is the best answer you could give in this particular situation and moment in time.

Accept the beliefs of the world-class impromptu speaker and your thinking speed on stage will increase at least 2 million times. Remember what the beliefs are? "I will not always give a stellar answer. I will begin speaking no matter what. My subconscious mind will suggest to me the best possible option for the answer at the moment I need it."

Yes and …

When you speak impromptu, time goes only forward and you can't change what you already said. If you say, "Oh, I am sorry. I didn't mean that" or "Forget about what I just said," it not only doesn't change what you just said but also makes your audience members think less of your speech.

They will think, "The speaker doesn't take what he is speaking about seriously and is wasting my time with meaningless excuses."

Imagine that after hearing a question, "Which animal is your favorite pet?" you respond, "I love dogs. When I was 7 years old my mom bought me a puppy, which I named Chip." At this moment, you remember a funny story about your friend's cat and want to change your response completely.

You may think, "What can I do in such a situation?" The most important thing is to accept what you said before and move forward. What you already said is a done deal and was important at the time you said it. Never apologize or say it was unimportant.

Make a quick transition from "dogs" to "cats" and continue your speech in a new direction. For example, "Dogs were truly my favorite pets until recently. A month ago my friend Jim said, 'Andrii, I am going to Hawaii for vacation. Can you please look after my kitten for 2 weeks?'" Next, I would tell my story and make a conclusion stating that cats are my favorite pets. With such a transition, your answer is very smooth and what you said about dogs sounds very naturally integrated into the overall response.

During an impromptu speech, you may change the direction of your answer several times, but make sure that you don't reject what you said earlier. Tell yourself, "Yes, I agree with everything said before and can continue my speech in any direction." You can switch easily between ideas using transitions and your speech will sound natural.

The rule of the first thought

The rule of the first thought says, "Once you hear a question, begin answering it based on the first idea that pops up in your head."

If you wait longer, your internal dialogue will turn on. You will think, "I can't figure out the best answer. This idea is not perfect. What will everybody think about me? Oh, the time is passing and I still don't know what to say." Internal dialogue will block your subconscious and activate slow analytical thinking. Eventually, it almost always will lead you to a poor impromptu answer.

By answering with your first thought, you block the conscious thinking and activate the subconscious super-fast idea generation.

Before you begin speaking, it is not necessary to come up with the entire answer. As a minimum, you only need a starting point. Answer based on the first thought and if you come up with a good idea later, it is always possible to change direction of your speech on the fly.

How do I find time for thinking?

The first 30 seconds

After you hear a question, always take 30 seconds to think about the answer. Not only will your reply appear thoughtful, but you also will let your subconscious mind process millions of ideas for the answer. This habit will make all your impromptu speeches significantly better.

Many speakers are afraid of speaking impromptu. They think, "I doubt that I will come up with a great answer within only 30 seconds."

You see, it is indeed difficult to come up with a great answer within only 30 seconds even for the world's best impromptu speakers. If you know the entire answer after you hear a question, that's great, but it might not happen every time. In fact, you have much more time than 30 seconds to think.

Remember that it's not mandatory to know the entire answer when you begin speaking. What you need to know is only a starting point, a first thought. You will have plenty of time to think about the rest of your answer later.

Think while you speak

The speed of your thinking is much faster than your speed of talking. While you talk about an idea, your brain generates new thoughts that will allow you to develop the idea you are talking about, or transition to another one.

When you are talking with your friend about the amazing food at the sea resort where you vacationed, a thought may pop into your head about something funny that happened during the tour to the waterfalls. You transition smoothly from talking about the food at the resort to telling the story about the tour. For your friend it sounds completely natural, and he or she might not know that the thought about the story came to your mind only a few seconds ago.

The same principle is highly applicable in impromptu speaking. When you talk about an idea, your creative brain is thinking really quickly and, depending on what thoughts come to your mind, you develop a current idea or transition to another one.

The best time for thinking is while you are talking because it is not limited. You can slow down the rate of your speech to give you even more time to think.

If you feel that you don't know what to speak about, just take a pause. A dramatic pause is totally acceptable. During a short pause, your brain will catch up and your audience won't even notice anything unusual.

Remember that your brain is many times faster than your words. While you talk, your brain is thinking about what to say next. If you feel that you need more time to think, just speak more slowly or pause.

Exercises for thinking on your feet

Exercise 1: Flow of consciousness

The goal of this exercise is to develop the ability to begin a speech on any topic at any place. If you are sitting in a room, driving a car or walking somewhere, just talk about everything you see, feel and think.

For example, as I am writing these lines I am sitting in New York's JFK airport waiting for my flight. Here is how a flow of consciousness may look to me: "Now I sit on a metal bench in the New York airport. In front of me I see a man that speaks Russian on the phone. He is probably speaking to his wife. There are about 5 hours before my flight. I will probably continue writing a book about impromptu speaking for another hour or two and then will look for a place to have lunch. Oh, why aren't there any outlets in the airport for passengers? My laptop battery will be completely discharged soon. Actually, I am very excited about my flight to Europe. Every time I fly anywhere I feel like the plane takes me to a completely different world with new acquaintances, new adventures and new life experiences."

Certainly, I can't call the last paragraph a great impromptu speech; however, it took me literally 0 seconds to create it, because I just wrote what came to my mind. The goal here is to forget about the content of your speech and just fill 2-3 minutes of time with your flow of consciousness.

This is perhaps one of the most important exercises in the entire book. Once you are able to consistently fill 2-3 minutes with flow of consciousness, you can give an impromptu speech on any topic.

Everything else you learn in this book will help you to make your speech effective, interesting and valuable. However, at this point it is very important to gain confidence that no matter what the question is you can always find words for the answer.

When you experience a tough situation in finding what to say, just say what you really are thinking about. The audience loves speakers who show their vulnerability and tell the truth. Be sincere and just say what is going through your mind.

Imagine that you are asked a question, "If you could make only one wish and you knew it would come true, what would it be and why?"

Using the skills acquired in the "flow of consciousness" exercise, I might start with the following, "Once I heard a question I almost answered with, 'I want peace everywhere in the world.' If I said that, I believe you guys would think well of me. But my inner voice screamed, 'I want a billion dollars. Oh, better yet I want to become the mayor of a city like New York.'

At the age of 22, I went through a leadership training course and one of the tasks was to get at least 50 signatures from unknown people on the street. After I got probably 20 signatures, I saw two 20-year-old girls sitting on a bench. I said, 'I plan to become the mayor of Kyiv and need to gather 100,000 signatures to participate in the elections. Would you sign here, please?' The response I got knocked me down and I still remember it. 'Are you kidding me? You will never become a mayor.'"

You see, I didn't know how to answer the question in the beginning, so I said what was on my mind. However, a few moments later the story about collecting signatures popped into my head and I transitioned to that story.

Sometimes a theme will come readily to your mind and you can simply introduce the topic, give your view on it, and proceed to building a speech. However, at other times you may not have any idea about how best to answer a question. In such a case just say what you think until you come up with an idea about what to speak about. Keep your mind focused on the thoughts and concepts that arise in your head. You will see new relationships among ideas and concepts as you speak.

Even if the thoughts you say out loud are not phenomenal, your audience might be much more interested in hearing them rather than apologies or filler words.

Exercise 2: Talk about an object for 5 minutes

The goal of the "talk about an object" exercise is to develop ease in associative speech. First, pick any object you see. Second, talk about this object to your partner for about 5 minutes. Describe its history, functions and applications, and say what you think about it. After some time, you will realize that you can speak for several minutes about any object. This skill will help you significantly in impromptu speaking.

Decide which question to answer

Every day we are asked dozens of questions that we answer directly. For example, "Andrii, do you want tea or coffee for breakfast?" "I would prefer tea," or "Andrii, what time is it now?" "It's half past eight." We are so used to giving direct answers that when we hear a question from the audience we tend to answer it directly because we think that it is the only option.

No one can force you to answer a particular question. Only you can decide what answer to give or whether to answer it at all. The possibilities are endless: you can answer a question directly, answer only part of the question, make a speech that has no relationship to the question, say "no comment" or just decide to answer later.

Great impromptu speakers are aware of all the options. If they answer a question directly, it is because they made a conscious decision to do so, not because they think it is the only option. If you want to grow as an impromptu speaker, you need to accept that there are no limitations for your speech. Your answer does not have to be clever, truthful, realistic or related to the question. The only rule is that you need to make a conscious decision about what question you are going to answer.

Imagine that you are asked, "If you could vote for the most outstanding person of the 20th century, who would you vote for and why?"

What are the first thoughts that pop up in your head? Most people instantly think about somebody famous they know from the 20th century and try to explain logically why this person is the most outstanding.

Be aware that there are many more directions for your answer and you need to make a conscious decision about your direction. Below you can find some of the options for your choice of the question.

Answer a question as you understand it

Very often a question is asked obscurely. For example, in the question, "If you could vote for the most outstanding person of the 20th century, who would you vote for and why?" the definition of an "outstanding person" is quite obscure.

For some people, this may be the person who came up with the greatest invention; for others, it may be the funniest comedian. You can handle such a question by defining how you understand it and then answering a question in your interpretation.

For example, "For me, the most outstanding person of the 20th century is the person who had the biggest impact on my life and without whom my life simply wouldn't be possible. It's my grandmother …"

First, you define what the most outstanding person means to you, then you give a speech about your grandmother.

Once you are asked a question with obscure terms, you might be tempted to think hard about what the questioner really meant. However, it is not important. Just explain how you understand the question and answer it as you understood it.

Pick a word from a context

"If you could vote for the most outstanding person of the 20th century, who would you vote for and why?" Take any word from the text of the question and talk about it.

For example, if you chose the word "vote" your answer might be, "When we try to decide who the most outstanding person in the 20th century is, or who the best candidate to become a president is, we vote. But is public voting the best way to make a selection?" Then you can talk about voting and alternative ways to make a decision. In this method, you can pick any word from the question and make a speech about it.

Answer any question you want

With a proper transition, you can give an answer to any question of your choice regardless of the question asked.

For example, "Andrii, if you could vote for the most outstanding person of the 20th century, who would you vote for and why?"

I can make a transition like "What is important today is not who the most outstanding person in the 20th century was, but, rather, if the current school education system will help our children to make the 21st century even more remarkable than the 20th" or "This reminds me of a conversation with my dad when I was 7 about who I wanted to become when I grow up."

If you use an appropriate transition you can literally, with one or two sentences, get to any topic you really want to talk about. Regardless of the original question, you can answer any question using this technique. Politicians use this technique during interviews and TV shows all the time.

Answer a part of the question

Imagine that you are asked, "Do you agree with the following quote by Max De Pree, 'The first responsibility of a leader is to define reality. The last is to say thank you. In between, the leader is a servant.'?"

You can just pick any part of the question you liked and answer it. For example, you could answer the question, "Do you agree that the leader is a servant?" Or, you could instead answer the question, "Do you agree that the first responsibility of a leader is to define reality?" It's not always mandatory to answer the question completely; you can decide just to answer partially.

As you can see, answering a question directly is only one option. Be aware that there are numerous other options and you can be creative in choosing a question for your impromptu speech. Remember, your only goal should be to choose a question consciously and give a valuable answer to your audience. If you feel that slightly altering a question will help you to deliver a more valuable answer to the audience and to change their perspective, do so.

Transitions

When giving an impromptu speech, you talk about your first idea, then transition to the second idea and talk about it, then you transition to the third one and so on. To make your speech sound smooth, you use special sentences that help to move from one idea to another. If you master transitions you will not only be able to go smoothly from one thought to another in your speech, but you also will be able to talk about any topic for hours without preparation.

If you want to take your impromptu speaking to the next level and create smooth transitions on your feet, you need to practice. The exercises below will help to dramatically improve your ability to create smooth transitions in impromptu speech.

Exercises for transitions

You can work on any exercises in this book with a partner or on your own. The exercises are very similar to what you will experience while speaking off the cuff in front of the audience. You should focus on one particular element at a time. The more you practice, the easier it will be for you to speak impromptu and the more fun you will have on stage.

Exercise 1: Linguistic pyramids

The goal of this exercise is to develop a skill of making quick analogies and generalizations.

Pick any object that you can see, for example a cup. An object can either be generalized to the higher class or be split into subclasses. The higher class for a cup is dishes. Dishes may include plates, glasses or bowls.

Let's split a cup into several different subtypes. For example, there can be a coffee cup, a teacup, an aluminum cup or a porcelain cup.

Now pick different objects and play with raising or lowering the class. Devote about 5 minutes to this exercise. It's enough time to improve a skill, but not get bored. Do you want to learn how linguistic pyramids can help during your next impromptu speech?

Imagine that a topic for your impromptu speech is a cup. Here is how you can answer: "There are cups made from glass, porcelain or aluminum. The most special for me are cups made from aluminum because they remind me of my trip to China, which is a world leader in aluminum production."

Or you can answer, "A cup is a dish from which it is very convenient to drink coffee or tea. When I was a kid I wished that all dishes were made from paper because it was my responsibility to wash dishes after a meal."

In the first example, we transitioned with the help of lowering a class from a cup to the trip to China. In the second example, we transitioned from a cup to responsibilities by generalizing. "Linguistic pyramids" is a great exercise that can help you to transition from any object to the idea or topic you want to talk about.

Exercise 2: How a donkey is similar to a table

The goal of this exercise is to learn how to create analogies between completely unrelated objects. First, pick an animate being and an inanimate object. Then explain how this animate being is similar to the inanimate object.

For example, both a donkey and a table have 4 legs. You can sit on a donkey and on a table. It's difficult to move both a stubborn donkey and a heavy table. Both a donkey and a table can't speak English. A farmer can own both a table and a donkey.

Pick several pairs of animate beings and inanimate objects and explain how they are similar as in the example above. Do this exercise for 5 minutes.

Exercise 3: Creative associations

Choose any object or term and explain what it associates with in your mind. For example, if I were doing this exercise, it might look like the following: money-banker, coffee-mother or vacation-beach. Don't spend too much time thinking. The first association that comes to your mind is the best one.

Let's see how it could be used in the impromptu speech, "When I think about coffee, I remember my mother because she makes the best coffee I have ever drunk." With such a transition, you can easily change a topic from coffee to your mother or mothers in general.

Or "I associate peace with beauty pageants because the contestants often say, 'My biggest dream is world peace.' I believe they say it because the judges like it and it gives them a better chance to win the pageant. What if everyone always told the truth? Would the world be a better place?"

With this transition, I moved from "peace" to a question, "Would the world be a better place if everyone told only the truth?" Now your entire impromptu speech can answer this question and it will sound very logical because of the transition.

Structure of the impromptu speech

Many speakers follow a structure while giving a prepared speech but speak without any plan at all during the Q&A section. If your speech doesn't have a structure, your listeners may get lost. If they get lost, they get irritated and stop listening.

All great speeches have the same structure: opening, body and conclusion. You can improvise within these 3 components; however, the basic structure is always fixed. Nevertheless, your off-the-cuff speech is unprepared so be creative within a basic structure.

Opening

The main purpose of the opening is to get the attention of the audience and to give a flavor of what to expect. There are numerous ways to begin an impromptu speech; however, below you can find 3 methods that have proven to be most effective.

Begin with a statement

You can begin a speech with a statement on your position or a startling statement. For example, "At the age of 9, I wanted to become a dancer. At the age of 19, I became a networking engineer. At the age of 26, I will become a dancer." The unusual statement draws the attention of the audience and gives a hint about the direction of your speech.

Start with a call back

A very powerful way to begin an impromptu speech is to call back to the common experience of the entire audience. Mention what a previous speaker said, an event that recently happened in the audience, or refer to a person who everyone in the audience knows.

Call backs make your speech very personal and special for the audience. People feel that your impromptu speech is just for them. Every time you use a call back, you may notice the reaction of the audience. It is so powerful that the audience almost always reacts.

Start with a story

Everyone loves hearing stories in movies, in reality shows or in speeches. When you hear a story, you can relive an episode from the life of its characters. When you begin a speech with a story, such an opening captures the audience members' attention and introduces them not only to your speech but also to the world of your story's characters.

For example, "Two years ago my college friend John called me and said …" or "Last summer, in London, I was invited to a Christmas party. That evening completely changed my attitude toward Argentine tango."

I am often asked, "Andrii, is the opening and conclusion any different in an impromptu speech compared with a prepared speech?"

Yes. Because an impromptu speech usually lasts 1-3 minutes, its components are significantly shorter than in a prepared speech. For example, an introduction and a conclusion may sometimes be only 1 sentence long. Because you think while you speak and may change the direction of your speech in the middle, occasionally the opening may have little relation to the rest of the speech, but the conclusion should always be relevant, strong and clear.

Body of the speech

In the body of your impromptu speech, always share a single point. Because the impromptu speech is usually really short, you can convey only one point effectively. If you try to convey 2 or more points, it's impossible to make a solid answer. You can convey other messages while answering further questions during the interview or a Q&A session. The more focused your answer, the stronger it is.

There are different strategies that impromptu speakers use to answer a question, but there are 3 frameworks that have proven to be the most effective. These frameworks are consistently used by the world's best impromptu speakers. Even if you answer questions using only these 3 frameworks, all your unprepared speeches will be at a very good level.

Conclusion

Conclusion is perhaps the most important part of the entire speech because what is said in the end is remembered best by the audience. If your speech is good, the last sentence is what your listeners will recite to their friends later.

Finish your speech with a statement and your audience will remember your point. Finish your speech with a call to action and your audience may do something differently after your speech. These are the two most commonly used ways to end a speech, and both have been proven effective for powerful impromptu speeches.

A conclusion needs to summarize the takeaway message of the speech and restate your point. The purpose of speaking impromptu is not to fill time, but to give value to the audience and share your unique perspective on the question. Don't hide behind clever and meaningless words. Any good off-the-cuff speech needs to have a clear point to be effective.

To be clear, your point needs to be less than 15 words long and should include a message that you want your audience to remember if they forget everything else you said. If your takeaway message is longer than 15 words, it is not clear for you, and if it's not clear for you there is no chance it will be clear for your audience.

One more thing ... Look for an elegant way to tie the conclusion to the beginning of the speech. If you manage to do so, your speech will sound solid and consistent.

3 magic impromptu speaking frameworks

If you are a general and lead an army into combat, you need to have a good strategy. During the actual battle, a lot can happen unexpectedly and you will have to make many decisions impromptu. If you make some bad decisions during the fight, you can still win, but if you don't have any strategy before the fight begins, it is almost impossible to win even with a great army. The same is true for impromptu speaking. If you want your answer to be world-class, you need to have a strategy for your speech.

Having analyzed thousands of great impromptu speakers, I figured out that the best impromptu speeches in all kinds of situations were constructed using the same 3 approaches. These 3 effective strategies were included in *Magic of Impromptu Speaking* system and work 100% of the time. They are different and are used in different cases, but all of them are essential for you to know as an impromptu speaker.

Tell a story

Do you remember the tale *Little Red Riding Hood* that you heard in childhood? Do you remember any PowerPoint presentation that you heard several years ago?

The reason why most of us remember the tale about *Little Red Riding Hood* but don't remember dry PowerPoint presentations lies in the secret of how our memory works.

People remember points of wisdom only when they are associated with stories that happened to them or that they have heard.

When we hear a story we can imagine a beach where the action takes place, hear how the characters talk and feel the emotions. Stories are easy to remember for a human brain as they evoke emotions and activate visual, auditory and kinesthetic senses.

If you tell a fact or make a point that is associated with a story, it may be remembered forever. If your points are very clever and interesting but are not associated with a story or a visual example, they may be forgotten right after you finish speaking.

Even a story that is not spectacular, well told or long can have a dramatic effect on how your point is remembered. Our brains remember information only in association with stories, visual examples or personal experiences.

Three years ago, I heard a story told by a woman over the phone during a webinar. The story was about a time when she worked as a nurse in a hospital while her city was bombarded during a war.

Vocal variety was far from great. There wasn't any conflict or clear conclusion, but even after several years, I can still retell this story in detail.

An inexperienced speaker who is making his or her first speech by telling a story is much more effective on stage than an experienced speaker who doesn't. This is how powerful stories are. If you remember just one thing from this book, I want it to be this: "Tell a story and associate it with a point."

In impromptu speaking, just as in prepared speaking, the most effective strategy is to tell a story and make a point. The best structure you can use on stage for the impromptu speech is opening, story and conclusion.

Stories help to eliminate the unexpectedness factor. The story happened in your life, you may have told it before, and while you are telling it on stage, you clearly know what the next sentence is. While your brain is freed from thinking about the next sentence, you can focus on pondering the conclusion.

Transition to a story from your life

Sometimes you can answer a question directly with one of the stories from your life. For example, "Please tell me about your first day of school." You can easily answer by telling a story about your first day of school.

However, very often you need a transition to go smoothly from the question that was asked to one of the stories that you remember.

When my wife and I lived in Santa Clara, California, I was a member of 7 Toastmasters clubs and visited many others as a guest. Toastmasters is an organization that gives speakers the opportunity to practice prepared and impromptu speeches in front of a live audience.

During one of the club meetings, I said to my wife, "Olena, let's bet that no matter what question is asked I can always answer it with the same story." That week I answered 7 different questions with the same story but different transitions.

If you have a certain amount of stories that you remember, you can transition to them from almost any question using phrases like, "This reminds me of" or "What is important today." Politicians often use a transition technique. They are asked different questions but with the help of a transition, they come to the topic they want to talk about.

Craft a fictional story on the go

Create an imaginary story to support your point. There is no limit to how creative you can be. You can say, "Imagine that" or "What if ..." and let your imagination go wild. Some of the best impromptu speeches I have ever heard used this approach. Try it. It's extremely effective and fun. Audiences love it.

For example, your speech may begin with, "I have never gone fishing, but I imagine that ..." Let your audience know that your imagination went wild and tell a tall tale. You don't necessarily need to tell the truth.

When you need to answer a question during a corporate meeting, you occasionally may find that telling a story is not appropriate. Sometimes you may decide to go with an easier approach than telling a story. For these situations, there are 2 other frameworks in the *Magic of Impromptu Speaking* system that you may find very handy.

PEEP

PEEP (Point, Explanation, Example and Point) is a very easy but effective and practical approach. If you struggle with finding an appropriate story for the answer, you can use this method. Use it when you need to give an opinion and back it up.

Point: Make a point in the opening of your speech.

Explanation: State your reasons for making this point in the body of the speech.

Example: Use an example or illustration to justify your previous remarks. Use words like "for example" or "imagine." Speaking about personal experiences will make your answer genuine and also memorable for your audience members.

Point: Drive home your point again. Link the conclusion to the opening.

As you can see, the first and the last "P" in PEEP serve as opening and conclusion. Explanation and Example fill the body of the speech. Example makes your point of view real and understandable for your listeners because just like a story, it activates the audience's senses in imagination. This approach is very popular among many impromptu speakers because it is very easy to apply.

Position, Action, Benefit

The Position, Action, Benefit approach is very useful when you report your findings to the board of directors or make a sales pitch to a CEO who has only 5 minutes to listen. I call this approach corporate because it is best suited for the corporate setting where telling a story might not always be appropriate and the decision needs to be made quickly. Your answer might not be remembered for years, but it will allow your audience to make an informed decision quickly.

For example, you may be asked, "Should we buy this company or not?", "How can your product help us?" or "Should we stop this project or continue it?"

Position: State your position on the question asked.

Action: Tell which action needs to be taken to implement your suggestion.

Benefit: Describe the benefit of your position.

If you answer a question using the position, action, benefit approach, your audience members will have all the information they need to make a decision.

Storytelling

Stories engage visual, auditory and kinesthetic senses of the audience. The day after your impromptu answer, the listeners won't remember any words you said; they will remember only what they saw, heard and felt in their imagination while you were speaking.

If you want your point to be remembered and have any impact, you need to associate it with a story or visual example. You may think, "Andrii, how can I tell an effective story that the audience will remember and enjoy?" You have told numerous stories to your family or friends about your vacation or what happened at work; however, for speaking impromptu effectively you need to learn the 3 foundations of storytelling.

Details tell a story

Stories are effective because they create scenes in the imagination of the audience. Use details to make the scenes real for your listeners.

Imagine that a speaker says, "I lost the first fight in a karate competition, but I enjoyed the experience." Is this phrase interesting for you? Is it memorable? Did it make you imagine the story?

Recall a final climax scene in a story, "The biggest secret of impromptu speaking."

"The fight lasted a minute and a half. I punched, kicked and made blocks, but most often I was punched. After 45 seconds I felt completely exhausted, like I couldn't even raise my hands, much less punch. The audience raved, "Andrii! Andrii! Kick his ass! Kill him!" When you hear your name cheered, it should give you more strength and power to win, but in my case it was the opposite. Guess what? My opponent's name was also Andrii! He had a green belt and more than 7 years of experience in karate. I lost that fight. I was beaten up. But it was truly fun! Few things can compare to it."

The second description of the same fight gives you much more detail. You know the background of my opponent in karate, who the audience supported, how long the fight lasted and how I felt during the fight. All these details make a story memorable. You will forget the words but will remember the scene that was drawn into the imagination by these words.

Details are the most important component of any story. Tell stories and make them detail-rich. This principle will make you a really good impromptu speaker. People like stories. People like details. People love speakers who know it.

Dialogue

If you don't use dialogue in a presentation, it's a news report, an article, a narration, but not a speech. Dialogue is an essential component of any story as it brings events of the past to life.

For example, "When I came home, I went to the kitchen, took several sheets of paper from my bag and started working on the problem. My reputation at school was at stake. At 1 a.m. my mom said, "Andrii, it's late. Go to bed. How is it going with that math problem, by the way?" "Mom, I see why nobody solved it before. It's insanely difficult. I tried everything and now have run out of ideas." This event happened many years ago, but a dialogue brings it alive and the audience can see how the story unfolds in real time.

All world-class impromptu speakers use dialogues in their speeches because they know that dialogue is a magical tool that makes a speech engaging, real, and memorable.

Every story is a combination of narration and dialogue, and your goal, as a speaker, is to find the right proportion. Most speakers have too little dialogue and too much narration in their impromptu speeches, so if you want to make your story engaging and memorable just increase the amount of dialogue in it. Dialogue is what turns an okay speech into an outstanding one.

Conflict

Conflict is a barrier between a character and what he or she wants to achieve. Conflict introduces an intrigue to a story and creates questions in the minds of the audience members. People are interested in hearing your story because they want to learn how the conflict will be resolved.

The structure of a story is introduction of the conflict, escalation of the conflict, and the resolution. As the impromptu speech is much shorter than a prepared one, you need to introduce a conflict very early, often in the first couple of sentences.

For example, "When I was about 12 years old, I had a huge fear. I was scared of being beaten up on the street by bullies. I was so afraid to go to school every day that my parents enrolled me in the Kiokushin Karate school to get this fear out of me."

Conflict can be a battle of man versus man, man versus difficulties, or even man versus himself. In this example, it is a battle of me against my fear.

Even if you use dialogue and details, the audience can still get bored listening to your speech without a conflict. Every great story, like a Hollywood movie, needs to have a conflict in the beginning that will be resolved later.

To make your story a blockbuster, introduce a conflict early in a story. Escalate it and once your audience is eager to know how it gets resolved, show the climax and give a resolution.

Your goal is to try to adhere to 3 fundamentals of the perfect story. Keep them in mind before you go on stage and you will notice how engaging your stories become for the listeners. Your audience members will think, "Wow! It is pure magic how this speaker can craft such outstanding stories after only 30 seconds of preparation." You, however, will know that this magic consists of 3 words: details, dialogue and conflict.

Exercises for storytelling

To become a well-rounded impromptu speaker you need to master the skill of telling stories. In impromptu speaking, you need to think really fast and decide how your story will unfold while you are telling it. As with any other skill, mastery in telling stories impromptu comes with practice. "Story-story," "nouns from the bag" and "complete a story" are excellent games that will polish your skill of telling stories while you have fun with friends or fellow impromptu speakers.

Exercise 1: Story-story

The goal of the "story-story" game is to develop a skill of talking about any topic. A moderator provides a setting for a story. He or she points at a person who begins telling a story. The moderator gives a signal to one of the participants and he or she continues the story from the place where the previous person stopped.

The new person picks up from the last word and tries to continue the narrative. Every speaker should have several turns to add to a story. Usually a moderator suggests when a story ends and asks one of the participants to make a conclusion.

Exercise 2: Nouns from the bag

In this exercise, participants write nouns on a slip of paper. Proper nouns are acceptable. In fact, the stranger the nouns, the more interesting this game will be.

After all the papers have been collected in a bag, one participant begins telling a story. After a storyline is established, the moderator picks a paper from the bag and a speaker includes this word in a story. For example, "Yesterday I went to a restaurant with my wife. It was our wedding anniversary and I wanted to make this afternoon special for us."

At this point the moderator picks the word "penguin" from the bag and a speaker continues the story. "The restaurant is called 'Antarctica' and they had a special dish of the day made from the meat of penguin. So I ordered it for both of us. I asked, 'Honey, do you remember how we met 10 years ago?'" Now the moderator picks another word from the bag and this continues until the story ends.

The game "nouns from the bag" develops on-the-spot thinking and the skill of crafting a story while you speak. As you can see, this exercise is very similar to what you face during the actual impromptu speech. You tell a story impromptu and every few seconds decide in which direction it will go.

Exercise 3: Complete a story

This exercise helps to develop the ability to craft an imaginary story with any setting. A participant should tell a story in the setting that the moderator announces.

For example:

"I received an anonymous text that said, 'I know where you are …'"

"The trail dead-ended into dense forest. A sign read, 'Enter at your own risk …'"

"While walking to the store I found an envelope. Inside was $10,000. I decided to …"

"A laid-back bike ride through the wilderness turned dangerous when out of nowhere jumped …"

"A knock on the passenger side window was startling. When I looked to see who it was …"

"The rain didn't show signs of stopping, but I had to …"

"It was the second time they called. This time I answered …"

You can play this game with only one partner or in a large group. Invent interesting introductions and let your imagination go wild. The more freedom you allow your imagination during the practice, the more it will help you later in impromptu speaking.

Take a stand

Take a stand. You need to have your particular point of view about a question asked. Imagine that you sit in the audience and a politician is asked a question, "Could you please tell us when we will get out of the economic crisis?"

A speaker answers, "It depends. If the government takes the right actions, we might get out of this crisis relatively quickly. However, if our nation doesn't unite and the government doesn't take the right steps to eliminate economic problems, the crisis may last much longer."

Neither answer gives any value nor will it be remembered or cited by the media. However, suppose the politician says, "I think that in 3 years we should get to the point of 2008 in our economy." Even if it's only an opinion that is not backed up by any data, it gives value, it will be cited by the news media, and it might be remembered for a long time.

One of the common mistakes that some speakers make is rattling off whatever comes to mind simply to fill up the time without making a stand. A good speech always has a message and a definitive point of view. Never be on the fence and never say "it depends."

Delivery techniques

Many speakers, after hearing a question, think, "Oh, the most important thing for me is to figure out what to say." How you deliver an impromptu speech, however, is much more important than what you say.

Be genuine

If you asked me, "What is the most powerful delivery technique in impromptu speaking?" I would say "Sincerity, for sure!" Many people want to be liked by the audience and play a role on stage. They want to show that they are knowledgeable like a Harvard professor, eloquent like Tony Robbins and charismatic like Steve Jobs.

The audience can see much more than you can only imagine through your nonverbal signals. Once your listeners feel that you are not genuine, they will stop trusting you and your speech will be over for them.

The audience members don't need another Tony Robbins, Steve Jobs or Martin Luther King. They need you. People will forgive anything on stage except insincerity. If you are truly genuine, your speech will be perceived well even if you mess up everything else.

Sometimes my students ask me, "Andrii, I want to be genuine on stage, but I don't know how. Is there any technique that can help me?"

You can't be genuine without perceiving your audience members as your best friends, without having fun speaking impromptu, and without intending to give value. There is a magical invocation that will ensure that your impromptu speech is always genuine and effective. It always works for me, for my students, for great impromptu speakers and for everybody who uses it. However, to make it work you need to truly believe in it. Before you go on stage repeat the following words, *"I will have fun from speaking impromptu and will enjoy every second of being on stage. People in the audience are the best people in my life. They are as important to me as my family or best friend. The only reason I am on stage is to give value and change the lives of my audience members for the better."*

Be energetic

Many years ago I attended an acting training led by a famous stage director. One of the students in my group was 21-year-old Julie. One day the trainer said, "Now it's time to give a 3-minute speech that you have been working on during the weekend. Julie, you are first." When Julie went on stage she smiled and said, "The title of my speech is 'Fashion trends of spring.' This season, the polka-dot dress is popular. I like the bright colors …"

I thought, "It's amazing! Julie didn't implement anything that the stage director taught us. Her speech doesn't have any structure, she stumbles a lot, the topic is not interesting for me, but her speech is awesome! I could listen to it for hours!"

I asked myself, "What is special about her speech?" And then I realized, "Julie is highly energetic and passionate about what she is talking about and it's contagious." This is perhaps one of the most valuable lessons I learned about public speaking in my life.

If you are passionate about your topic, your energy is contagious and very soon everyone in the audience will be excited. They will think, "Wow, there could be something special about this topic since the speaker is that excited. I should listen." On the other hand, if the audience members see that you are indifferent, they will become bored and indifferent, just like you.

Being energetic is one of the foundations of the successful impromptu speech. No matter what you are talking about impromptu, be excited about it and speak with energy and passion. When the energy of excitement spreads throughout the room it's magic and you are the wizard.

Gestures

When you look at some beginner impromptu speakers, you may notice that they occasionally stare at the ceiling or make nervous gestures. Why? The brain is busy figuring out what to say and a speaker tends to forget completely about gestures and eye contact.

When you are on stage, you might think that the biggest problem is to find the right words because the audience might judge your speech based on what you say. However, the audience also judges your speech based on what you do on stage while you are thinking or speaking. If you are fidgeting with your fingers, dancing from one leg to another or staring at the ceiling, it not only looks irritating, but also makes your listeners doubt your confidence in what you say.

The expectations for gestures and movements on stage are usually lower for impromptu than for a prepared speech, but you need to adhere to some basic best practices.

Just like in a prepared speech, all your gestures should be broad and open. You should always look directly into the eyes of one of the audience members and of course avoid all kinds of nervous gestures.

You may think, "How can I control so many things on stage? I should think about what to say, control my eye contact, movements and gestures. Isn't it too much?" The answer to this question relates to the foundation of thinking on your feet.

If you try to think consciously about your content, gestures, eye contact and movements, you will easily get overwhelmed. Your goal is to not think about all these things! Your goal is to trust your super-fast subconscious mind.

If you asked me, "How do you control your gestures?" I would say, "They just happen. I trust my subconscious and it gives me signals of when to gesture and how to gesture. The same happens when you walk. Your subconscious gives you a signal when to make a movement and you make it without thinking."

When you practice speaking impromptu at a Toastmasters club or in a circle of friends, ask whether you make any kind of irritating gestures and whether you make proper eye contact. Eliminate the mistakes one by one in your subsequent speeches. After a certain amount of practice all your gestures, movements and nonverbal signals will be good even without thinking about them.

Fear of impromptu speaking

I have interviewed more than 100 speakers and all of them have said that they do feel fear of speaking impromptu. I asked, "Is there anything particular that you fear?" and received the following responses, "I fear that I will not be able to create a great answer quickly" and "I am afraid that the audience will not like my answer and will think badly of me." In fact, all speakers, to a certain degree, fear speaking impromptu. It is easy to reduce fear of impromptu speaking significantly if you follow the 3 recommendations below.

Rely on your previous experience

If you fear impromptu speaking, you are not alone. People fear everything that is unfamiliar to them. Every time you get out of your comfort zone you feel fear, but it is also the time you grow the most.

When I was 7 my mom said, "Starting Monday you will go to school on your own." I said, "Mom, I am very afraid to go to school without you. I haven't gone anywhere by myself before. I am afraid that I will get lost."

Guess what? I felt fear only the first day I went to school without Mom. However, I then realized that I did remember the path, I had gone to school already many times before, and there was nothing to fear. The same happens to every impromptu speaker.

After you give more than a dozen answers impromptu and practice the techniques of thinking on your feet, you will think, "Hey, I have spoken impromptu before! Sometimes my answers were great, sometimes they were so-so, but it wasn't as bad as I feared. The audience didn't eat me alive and I even had fun."

To reduce fear of impromptu speaking, just make it familiar to you and it will become a part of your comfort zone. Speak impromptu as often as you can and after a while you will not fear it anymore. Why? Because you already spoke impromptu and know from your previous experience that there is nothing to fear.

Accept that not every answer will be stellar

Realize and accept the fact that not all of your impromptu answers will be stellar. Many circumstances are difficult to predict, such as the question you will get, ideas you will have, what your mood will be, and who will be in the audience.

The best impromptu speakers know that it is impossible to give stellar answers consistently. Once you accept this fact you not only will stop worrying that your answer won't be good, but you also will give much better answers on average. Your subconscious mind won't be blocked by your worries and will give you great ideas for a speech.

Get familiar with the setting

If you anticipate that you might speak impromptu, get familiar with the setting. To allow your brain to think only about the answer, eliminate the elements that are unfamiliar to you and that can provoke unnecessary fear.

Get on stage and look at the empty audience seats. Sit in different corners of the room. Shake hands and speak with the audience members. The better the connection you feel with the room and the people, the easier it will be for you to think on your feet and connect with the audience.

Once you go on stage, the room will be familiar to you and the audience members will be your allies. You will speak to the audience just as you would to a group of friends in your kitchen. Without fear of the unfamiliar setting and the audience, your brain will concentrate only on thinking about the answer.

Most people fear impromptu speaking, but experienced impromptu speakers know its nature and how to reduce it.

Humor

When you speak impromptu, humor may be more important than during the prepared speech. Humor creates a relaxed atmosphere in the audience and puts your listeners at ease while listening.

Good humor can make your audience enjoy your speech more. Good humor can make the audience listen attentively and remember everything you say better. Good humor can make you win an impromptu speaking competition. To use humor effectively, you need to understand what makes people laugh and how to make your speech funnier.

The structure of the joke

Any joke consists of two parts: a setup and a punch line. A setup is the background information that the audience needs to know for a humorous line to be funny.

The punch line is a humorous line that makes the audience laugh. The setup is where the pattern is established and everything goes in the same direction. The punch line is where a train of thought is derailed from a pattern and people laugh. We laugh when our mind is tricked successfully.

For example, "In the 21st century we have an iPhone, an iPad, but no eye contact." In this case "iPhone" and "iPad" set the pattern and the audience expects something like an "iPod" to be next. "Eye contact" derails the sequence from the pattern and makes the phrase funny.

Another example is, "Do you know the most effective way to convey information? Telegraph? No. Telephone? No. Tell a woman!" In this case, "telegraph" and "telephone" set the pattern and "tell a woman" is the punch line.

In order for a punch line to be funny, the setup should be known to the audience. If you told a joke in your circle of friends and they were dying from laughter but it didn't have any effect during the presentation you made at work, it means that the first audience knew a setup but the second one didn't.

Exaggeration and Dialogue

My student George once asked, "Andrii, I want to make people laugh but it's quite difficult for me to come up with humorous lines. How can I be funnier while speaking impromptu?"

I said: "George, it's very easy. There is a magical source of humor that can give your speeches an endless amount of funny moments if you know about it. Dialogue and exaggerations are this magical source."

When you speak impromptu, in the majority of cases, people laugh either when you say a dialogue line of the character in your story, or when you show an exaggerated reaction of another character to this line.

If you just add more dialogue and exaggerated reactions there will be enough humor in your speech. Even if you didn't intend for your dialogue lines or exaggerated reactions to be funny, often people will laugh anyway.

My analysis of thousands of speeches shows that dialogue and exaggerations contain many more funny moments for the audience than other parts of the speech. Use the magic source of humor and you will notice that your audience members laugh much more often than before.

An impromptu speech needs to be succinct

Usually an impromptu speech is only 1-3 minutes long and you need to be succinct in order to convey your message and to make it crisp. Each word that you say either adds or detracts value from your speech and there is no middle ground. Following the recommendations below will significantly reduce the amount of unnecessary words in your speeches.

Avoid filler words

Avoid filler words such as "um," "ah," "basically," "you know," etc. These words just irritate the audience and don't add any value. If you don't know what to say or just feel nervous, instead of using a filler word take a pause to give yourself a couple of seconds to think.

Don't apologize

Never say "Sorry," "I don't know much about this topic" or "Sorry, I just didn't want to say that." When you apologize on stage, you waste your audience's valuable time and it is quite rude. To apologize in our everyday life is a sign of politeness, but you need to forget about the word "sorry" when you speak impromptu. Never apologize for not knowing the subject because if you are not qualified to speak, why should the audience listen to you?

Your impromptu speech shouldn't be perfect. If you stumbled or said something you didn't want to say, just continue speaking.

Condense stories

Telling a story is a very effective way to answer a question, but for an impromptu answer you need to shorten it.

If you have several events in a story, condense them into the most important one. If you have different characters that are necessary to convey a message, condense the number to 2 or 3. Condense the conversation of the characters to only those phrases that are relevant to your point.

By condensing events, conversations and characters, you will be able to answer a question impromptu with a 2-minute story that usually takes 10 minutes to tell and still convey a point.

Be simple

When you speak impromptu, your vocabulary should be at a level that a 12-year-old kid could understand. Public speaking has changed dramatically over the last 50 years. Great speakers of the past such as Winston Churchill or Abraham Lincoln used long sentences, advanced vocabulary and eloquent words, but the greatest speakers of today use much simpler language in their speeches.

A good impromptu speaker needs to be genuine on stage and speak to the audience just as he or she would speak to a friend in everyday conversation. Today people speak in short sentences and use simple language in everyday communication. This is reflected in public speaking, too.

Very often I see speakers who either try to hide their incompetence behind professional terms and abbreviations or try to speak eloquently to look better than they actually are. Unfortunately for them, if the audience notices that a speaker is not genuine, they stop listening to the speech and trusting the speaker.

The greatest experts, leaders and speakers can always explain the most difficult concepts with very simple words and visual examples that even a 12-year-old kid can understand.

If a 12-year-old kid can't understand what you mean, then an engineer with two university degrees won't either. Believe me, an engineer in the past, with two university degrees, who has heard thousands of technical presentations.

If you want to be an effective impromptu speaker and make your speech valuable for the audience, be simple.

Don't strive to be perfect

In impromptu speaking, a perfect speech is a terrible speech. If your speech is very well polished and doesn't have any flaws, your audience will notice that you reproduced the rehearsed text instead of having a genuine conversation with the audience. People like imperfection. They want to see an imperfect, real you.

The expectation for flawlessness in your impromptu speech is much lower than for a prepared speech. Often you will notice that even without a great idea for the answer, without a relevant opening, and with several stumbles, your speech still will be considered great by the audience.

The biggest danger in unprepared speaking lies not in mistakes but in your striving to always give a perfect answer. It blocks quick thinking on your feet, stymies your ability to take risks on stage and lowers your confidence. If you want to become a better impromptu speaker – take risks, forget about being perfect and enjoy your experience on stage.

4 Levels of World-Class Impromptu Speaking

Let's imagine that impromptu speaking is a computer game. This game has 4 levels of difficulty, which you need to go through one by one. After finishing the first 3 levels you will become a really good impromptu speaker, but only after passing the final 4th level will you become one of the best impromptu speakers in the world. Are you ready to play? Let's begin.

Level 1: Speak for 2 minutes

At this level you need to overcome the brain freeze when your mind is going blank and become confident that you can easily speak for 2 minutes on any topic without preparation.

The first level is basic but the most fundamental one. At this level, your only goal is to speak about anything for 2 minutes. Don't worry about whether what you say makes sense. Don't worry about structure or delivery. The only goal is to fill 2 minutes with speaking.

Have you ever seen speakers who stumble and get embarrassed while answering a question impromptu? These speakers still haven't passed through level 1. No matter how experienced you are, if you are working on polishing your level 1, forget about the quality of your speech and just fill the time with words.

Once you are very comfortable on level 1, you will never be afraid to speak off the cuff because you will know that no matter what question is asked you will find the words to answer it somehow. Other levels will ensure that your answer is spectacular but first you need to get rid of the fear that you won't find words once you need them.

You can only eat an elephant piece by piece. The same is true for impromptu speaking. Before you have mastered a previous level, don't try to go to the next one and get confused with too many techniques at once. Only once you are absolutely confident with the first level should you move on to level 2.

Level 2: Add structure and sense

Your listeners can remember information and follow your thoughts only if you speak in a structured way. From a high-level perspective, your speech should have an introduction, body and conclusion. At this level you need to be able to use the frameworks easily for structuring your response. In addition, your speech should support a particular point of view and what you speak about should be clear to the audience. While working on this level, don't pay attention to the body language, vocal variety or eye contact. You will have an opportunity to work on all of these on level 3.

Level 3: Delivery

Most of the delivery techniques used in long speeches are applicable for an impromptu speech. On level 3 you should work on gestures, pauses, eye contact, vocal variety and other delivery techniques. The aim of this level is to develop the ability to deliver an impromptu speech with power, passion and charisma. After you finish working on level 3 all your impromptu answers will be perceived well by the audience.

Level 4: Slant

If you feel comfortable with the first three levels, you are already an advanced impromptu speaker. Congratulations! However, to get to the point where your speeches are remembered for years, you need to master level 4.

There are many good impromptu speakers, but very few are great. If you participate in an impromptu speaking competition, all of the contestants are good speakers, but level 4 is what differentiates a winner from the rest. If you see that your impromptu answer is remembered for years after you gave it, then your speech was at level 4.

If your answer is obvious and doesn't have a unique perspective on the question, it's boring and the speech will be quickly forgotten. Your audience can't concentrate on anything that is boring. You need to avoid giving predictable answers and give your speech a slant (unexpected twist).

For example, suppose you are asked, "Where would you like to spend your next vacation and why?" First, think about the most obvious answers that the majority of people would give, such as "I want to go to Mexico and spend some time at the beach because I am very tired at work and just need to relax," "I want to go skiing in Canada with my family. I enjoy skiing and spending time with family is the best vacation for me" or "I will travel around Europe because I enjoy sightseeing and meeting new people."

In a personal conversation such answers will do fine, but you can't answer like that if you want your impromptu speech to be at level 4. Your audience doesn't care about your vacation but cares about what value they can get from your response. Value is your unique life experience, good laughter or unusual point of view.

Once you have decided for yourself what the most obvious answers could be, take your speech in a completely different direction.

For example, "I would like to spend my entire vacation in the office …" "I would go to jail for 2 weeks …" "In my life every day is a vacation because …" "I'd like to fly to the moon with Ricky Martin for a week …" or "I would like to be invisible during my vacation so that …" These beginnings of the answer are unusual and will intrigue your audience to hear more.

It's true that very few speakers are at level 4, but it is not difficult at all to get to this level. When you speak in front of the audience, it's not a private conversation anymore and your goal is not to say what you really think but to give value.

Be creative, avoid predictable directions and your speeches will be remembered for years. People will be looking forward to each of your impromptu speeches. Why? Because they will think, "This speaker is awesome. I am intrigued to hear what he will say this time." When you take a stand that is different from the rest, people will notice you.

Additional tips

The tips in this section are as important as the others in the book, but they don't fall into any of the other sections.

Make it a priority to understand a question

Don't answer a question you don't understand. It is better to ask a second time or even a third time rather than to ramble and give a poor answer.

If you speak impromptu in front of a large audience, once you hear a question rephrase and repeat it. By doing so you let everybody hear the question and acknowledge that you understood it.

Acknowledge the importance of the question

If you give impromptu answers during a Q&A session, occasionally say, "That's a very good question" if you really think so.

At the end of your answer you also can ask, "Does that answer your question?" to make sure that you answered a question sufficiently. These phrases connect you with your audience because they show that you not only listen to people, but also hear them and care that they get good answers.

Time yourself

Make sure that your answers are brief and don't exceed 3 minutes on average. If your answers are long, people will be afraid to ask further questions because they don't want to prolong the presentation significantly if they are seeking to leave on time.

The longer you speak, the more likely you are to lose the attention of the audience. After 2 minutes, it is more and more difficult to keep your audience engaged and excited about the answer.

No matter how much you know about the subject, avoid giving impromptu answers that are longer than 5 minutes. Suggest discussing a topic in more detail either during the break or the next time. Long responses may be irritating and boring for the audience. Impromptu answers are supposed to be short.

Personalize your speech

When you give an impromptu answer, your personal experience and perspective hold more value than facts, statistics or any information that is available on the internet.

Your audience members want to learn your experience, little-known facts and your unique perspective. You, as a speaker, are interested in giving value to the listeners and making their lives better by your answer.

Make your speech as personal as possible to connect with the audience and to make it world class. Refer to the audience, use examples from your personal life and talk about issues that are important to the people who listen to you. Generic, dry answers never achieve anything besides boring the audience. Personal answers are remembered for years and sometimes have the power of changing lives.

Visualize your impromptu speech

A study was done a while back with Olympic runners and visualization. The runners were split into two groups, those who practiced for several hours a day and those who split the same amount of hours between practicing and visualizing themselves running.

The results were astonishing. Those runners who practiced without visualization showed very little improvement in their times, but those who mixed visualization with their training showed great improvement over their previous times.

Michael Jordan visualized not only games, but also winning. This allowed him to win game after game during his extraordinary career. Visualization techniques also work amazingly well in impromptu speaking.

Before coming on stage, visualize yourself giving an outstanding impromptu speech. Clearly imagine the smiles and applause of the audience. Imagine how great it will feel when you succeed. Your thoughts will send the signal to your subconscious and it will make your imagined scene a reality.

It's difficult to describe how the law of positive visualization functions from a scientific point of view, but it works for the greatest athletes, it works for the greatest impromptu speakers, and it will certainly work for you.

Where to find material for impromptu speeches?

Your answer depends not only on your impromptu speaking skills but also on your life experiences. The stories you tell, the examples you provide, and points you make are taken from the life you have lived, and the more versatile it is, the more interesting and valuable your impromptu speeches are.

Remember that people come to hear you primarily because of your unique life experience, not because you have great gestures or vocal variety. It is relatively easy to significantly increase the number of potential stories and experiences in your life that can be used later in impromptu speaking if you develop the right habits.

People tend to stick to routines and spend most days the same way. Because of this, when you are meeting your old friend or a schoolmate and ask, "Hey, haven't seen you in ages. What's happened in the last 5 years?" you may hear a response such as, "Nothing special. I work at the same company. Family is doing fine. We plan to go to Mexico for vacation in the summer." When you change patterns in your life and do what you have never done before, your new experiences result in interesting stories. Here are the habits of world-class impromptu speakers.

Go to places you have never been to before

First of all, travel. Go to other countries, states or cities. Some of the greatest memories of your life may come from travelling. When you change the environment, some of the greatest adventures of your life happen.

Go to an unusual restaurant that you have never been to. If you are not a football fan, go to a football game. If you have never been to a salsa dance party, visit one. If you have never had an interest in art – go to an art gallery.

After such experiences, you might not become a fan of football, salsa or art, but going to a place you have never been before will give you great new ideas that are invaluable not only for impromptu speaking but also for having an interesting and versatile life.

Try new experiences

Try new experiences and activities at least once in your life. If you have never played golf, driven a motorcycle or danced tango, try it once. You shouldn't become an expert in all the activities, but having tried those things at least once will give you great material for future impromptu speeches. Moreover, your perspective on the activity as a person who is trying it for the first time certainly will be fresh, interesting and sometimes hilarious.

Meet new people

In modern society, we tend to limit our communication to only those people we already know. However, a new person can open a new world for you. New acquaintances can bring great new opportunities or ideas into your life, which may be invaluable material for your future impromptu speeches.

When you fly in an airplane, try to start a conversation with the person sitting next to you. Talk to people in a bar, a museum or an art gallery. You never know what this new connection can lead to and what you can learn from any particular person.

Once I had a conversation with a man who is a co-owner of a big boxing magazine and was a professional boxer in the past. I learned so much about boxing and publishing that day. On another occasion, I talked with a guy in a bar whose hobby is fire swallowing. Had I not started the conversation with these people I would never know much about boxing or fire swallowing.

Read books

Books are the quickest and cheapest way to get an education in any area. I think books are very much underestimated in society in terms of the value they can give a reader. You can read a distilled experience that the author gathered for decades within several hours. The core idea here is to read books about areas you know nothing about. Most important for impromptu speaking is not the depth of your knowledge but its versatility.

Having developed the habit of doing what you have never done before will bring you such an amazing pool of interesting ideas and experiences that you will never struggle with finding something interesting to talk about in your impromptu speech. You need to live an interesting life to be an interesting impromptu speaker and an interesting person to talk to.

Stages of learning

Psychologists have researched how adults learn and figured out that adults learn new skills by going through the same 4-stage process. Impromptu speaking is not an exception. In order to truly become a world-class impromptu speaker, you need to go through the entire process.

Unconscious incompetence

Unconscious incompetence is a stage at which you just don't know what you don't know. I may ask you, "Is it easy for you to speak impromptu?" Your response may be totally confused because you never spoke impromptu before and you don't know whether it is difficult.

You may say, "Oh, it is not that difficult because I speak easily without preparation with my friend and I think speaking in front of an audience is pretty much the same."

Conscious incompetence

After you give your first impromptu speech you may think, "Oh, it's much more difficult than I thought. My mind went blank when I needed it the most, I didn't come up with any reasonable answer, I stumbled and felt miserable on stage."

This is a stage of conscious incompetence where you realize what you don't know. Only at the stage of conscious incompetence can you look for resources to learn a new skill. For example, you may decide to sign up for a training, buy a book or ask a more experienced friend for advice.

Conscious competence

After reading this book, you will be at the level of conscious competence. You consciously know all the techniques that will make you an effective impromptu speaker. Once you go on stage and implement new strategies for speaking off the cuff, you see initial results but also experience failures. You may struggle to remember all the techniques and occasionally you may implement them awkwardly.

The level of conscious competence is very dangerous. If you leave your skill at this level, with time you will forget all the knowledge you acquired and may stay at the same level you were before reading the book or trying new techniques. To truly master impromptu speaking or any other skill, you need to get it to the level of unconscious competence.

Unconscious competence

After you have thoroughly practiced the new impromptu speaking techniques that you learned in the book, they will become part of you. You will not need to remember anything you read because you will know it on a subconscious level. Speaking impromptu will be as natural for you as brushing your teeth or walking.

Imagine that you see in the eyes of your audience members that they enjoy your speech but you didn't put much effort into it. How does it sound? Few things can be more fun than speaking impromptu in front of a large audience.

I want you to become an outstanding impromptu speaker who can change lives and whose speeches are remembered for years. However, for my wish to come true you need to raise your impromptu speaking skill to the level of unconscious competence and for this you need to practice.

Where to practice?

If you want to become a great impromptu speaker, knowing the greatest techniques is not enough. You need practice to internalize them. You may ask, "Andrii, where can I safely practice speaking impromptu?" Actually, there are several great options.

Toastmasters clubs

Toastmasters International is an educational organization that runs more than 128,000 clubs worldwide intended to develop public speaking skills of its members. A typical session of the Toastmasters club involves giving prepared speeches, an evaluation section and a table topics session.

During the table topics session members of the club give impromptu speeches that last for 1-3 minutes. Toastmasters club is a unique place where you can practice new impromptu speaking techniques in a safe environment. No matter how you screw up on stage, you will hear applause and words of encouragement.

I highly recommend that you read more about Toastmasters at www.toastmasters.org, find a nearby club and visit it as a guest to decide if you want to become a member later. Once you are a member, volunteer to speak impromptu as often as possible.

With partners

Find a partner and practice together answering different questions impromptu. It really may be a very interesting way to spend time together and have fun. Try doing various exercises from this book in a pair or a group. Let your partner give you feedback about what you did great and how you could have improved your answer.

Practice alone

Practice impromptu speaking exercises on your own. They will greatly prepare you for actual impromptu speeches. When you are in a car, when you are walking or sitting in an armchair, pick an exercise or a question and try to speak for 2 minutes.

To grow very fast in impromptu speaking you need more practice. Practicing alone might not be as effective as in a group, but you can practice alone as much as you want and it is still effective.

After having answered several dozens of questions impromptu, you will notice that you are entering into the high-performance state faster, that topics repeat themselves, and that your answers get better and better because you have mastered the fundamental techniques.

Train your brain to answer impromptu questions as often as possible and you will notice that you are looking forward to the next opportunity to speak off the cuff because you are good at it and it is fun.

Final Checklist

Five minutes before you have to speak impromptu, it's difficult to go through the entire book or remember all the articles you have ever read to make sure you implement the best techniques. However, it is possible to go through a short checklist. Below you can find my checklist that I go through before going on stage.

1. Use the rule of the first thought.

2. Add an unusual slant to the answer.

3. Be genuine.

4. Be energetic.

5. Tell details.

6. My audience members are the best people in my life and my goal is to change their lives for the better.

7. Impromptu speaking is a game. I will have fun on stage.

Most speakers come on stage without keeping anything in mind and hope for luck. Seven is a lucky number and I am sure if you keep this checklist in mind you will be lucky on stage every time you speak and your speech will be outstanding.

Let's put everything together

Imagine that you won $1M in a lottery. How would you spend it?

One night, two years ago, I had a vivid dream. I was sitting in a huge boardroom at an oak table. If you were standing behind me, you could see Warren Buffett sitting across the table and looking right into my eyes.

"Andrii, imagine that Bill Gates gave you one million dollars. What would you spend it on?"

"I would travel around the world for 6 months on a luxurious yacht."

"Andrii, why didn't you make this trip yet?"

"Well, Warren, I don't have $200,000 to buy a yacht."

"Andrii, you don't need to buy a yacht for the trip, you can rent it. I think renting it for 6 months will cost about $20,000. I have never heard of anyone going on such an adventure alone. Find 10 like-minded people who share your dream and split the costs with them.

You see, you need only $2,000 now to fulfill your dream instead of $200,000. If you clean toilets for several months, you can save enough money to make your dream a reality.

If you really wanted to go on this trip you would have found opportunities to do so. I don't believe that you want to travel around the world badly enough."

At that moment I woke up. I couldn't forget about the dream for several months. I thought, "Warren was right. I don't want a trip around the world on a yacht. Everything I wanted badly enough in my life I already have."

I'd like to say, "Bill Gates, once I have a burning desire for something I will find the money and opportunities myself. Give a million dollars to somebody who needs it more than I do. What I really need is more worthy dreams that I want badly enough."

Now read the speech again but with comments about how the principles described in the book are applied in this short impromptu speech. It's not only important to know the techniques but also to see how they are applied.

Imagine that you won $1M in a lottery. How would you spend it? (With comments)

One night, two years ago, I had a vivid dream. I was sitting in a huge boardroom at an oak table. If you were standing behind me you could see Warren Buffett sitting across the table and looking right into my eyes. *(The details make a scene more vivid in the imagination of the audience.)*

"Andrii, imagine that Bill Gates gave you one million dollars. What would you spend it on?" *(I slightly alter a question to one I really want to answer. Instead of answering a question about how I will spend one million dollars won in a lottery, I am answering a question about how I will spend money given by Bill Gates.)*

"I will travel around the world for 6 months on a luxurious yacht." *(Dialogue makes the speech real for the listener as the action in a*

316

story unfolds in real time. You can not only learn about what Warren told me but also experience it yourself.)

"Andrii, why didn't you make this trip yet?"

"Well, Warren, I don't have $200,000 to buy a yacht."

"Andrii, you don't need to buy a yacht for the trip, you can rent it. I think renting it for 6 months will cost about $20,000. I have never heard of anyone going on such an adventure alone. Find 10 like-minded people who share your dream and split the costs with them.

You see, you need only $2,000 now to fulfill your dream instead of $200,000. If you clean toilets for several months, you can save enough money to make your dream a reality.

If you really wanted to go on this trip you would have found opportunities to do so. I don't believe that you want to travel around the world badly enough."

At that moment I woke up. I couldn't forget about the dream for several months. *(I decided to present my story in the form of a dream. In a dream you can make your imagination go wild and nobody in the audience will wonder how you met Warren Buffett in person, flew to Mars or led a platoon of ninja turtles into battle.)*

I thought, "Warren was right. I just don't want a trip around the world on a yacht. Everything I wanted badly enough I already have." *(Here my thoughts are presented in the form of a dialogue.)*

I'd like to say, "Bill Gates, once I have a burning desire for something I will find the money and opportunities myself. Give a million dollars to somebody who needs it more than I do. What I really need is more worthy dreams that I want badly enough."

(Here the conclusion ties to the beginning of the speech, which makes it circular. I take a stand and make clear what I will do in case Bill Gates offers me $1M. You can also see an unusual twist in the speech.

Most people would say, "I would buy a Ferrari or I would donate money to charity," but I took an unusual direction and said that I would refuse the money. Remember, a slant is required to make a speech memorable.)

As you can see the speech has a structure: opening, body and conclusion which makes it easier for the audience to follow and remember. The question was answered with a story, which evokes pictures in the imagination.

Also, as you can see, the vocabulary used in the speech is at a level that a 12-year-old kid can understand. As this impromptu answer is only 2 minutes long the story is succinct. Right from the beginning it gets to the core action and the point of the speech.

When you listen to the answers of other speakers at Toastmasters, on Youtube or at a corporate meeting, try to evaluate them silently based on the principles described in the *Magic of Impromptu Speaking* system. By evaluating others, you will learn the principles faster yourself.

Don't stop until…

I don't know how it happened but in 7th grade I passed the entrance exams into one of the best schools for math in the Ukraine. Six months later my mom was standing in the office of my algebra and geometry teacher, Alexander.

"Victoria, your son's performance is very poor. Honestly, I think math isn't his thing. It would be better for Andrii if you transfer him to another school at the end of the year."

In the afternoon I saw my mom crying, "Andrii,I graduated from school with distinction, your grandma graduated from school with distinction. Why are you studying so badly? I have been explaining basic math to you for hours, but you don't remember a thing. You could end up becoming a street cleaner."

When I was 12 years old, I didn't care about my grades. I didn't care about getting a higher education and I didn't care about my future. I knew only one thing, "If I don't like doing something, I'll avoid it by all means and studying at school is one of those things." I would probably have become a street cleaner if not for one event.

One day Alexander gave us an algebra problem for homework. I obviously couldn't solve it and went to my mom for help. After about 10 minutes, she explained the solution to me.

During the next lesson, Alexander told the class, "Please raise your hand if you have solved the problem I gave you last time." No one besides me raised their hand. "All right, Andrii, please solve the problem on the blackboard."

After I explained the solution Alexander said, "Andrii, Andrii ... You solved the problem that even the best students in the class couldn't. I respect you for this. You are cool."

I didn't solve the problem myself, but I enjoyed the feeling of being in front of the class and getting recognition from Alexander. Never before had I felt so good.

Starting that day, there weren't any problems I couldn't solve. Alexander called me to the blackboard only for the problems that nobody else solved. I was looking forward to the toughest problems because I knew that I would be called to the blackboard and would experience my minute of fame again.

I didn't do well in other subjects, but now math became my thing. It actually became my life. I did math at home, I did math during literature classes, and I did math while sleeping. Sometimes I woke up to write down the solution to a problem that came to me in a dream.

One day when we were studying the arithmetic progressions, Alexander gave us a problem, "Please calculate the sum of the row $(1^2+2^2+3^2+4^2...+n^2)$. By the way, in my career there was no student who solved this problem." Can you imagine what I was thinking?

When I came home, I went to the kitchen, took several sheets of paper from my bag and started working on the problem. My reputation at school was at stake. At 1 a.m. my mom said, "Andrii, it's late. Go to bed. How is it going with that math problem, by the way?"

"Mom, I see why nobody solved it before. It's insanely difficult. I tried everything and now just ran out of ideas."

For the next 4 weeks I was living at that table when I wasn't at school or sleeping. Now I clearly remember that table, I clearly remember the shirt I wore and I clearly remember that the solution I came to eventually took 5 sheets of paper. This problem was clearly one of the biggest challenges in my life.

After I shared my solution with the class, Alexander said, "Andrii, that's really impressive. You solved a problem that no student in my career within the last 25 years solved. I respect you. You are a warrior."

Eugen, the guy who sat behind me, whispered, "Sedya (my nickname at school), why are you so stupid, but so good at solving math problems?"

Alexander asked me, "Andrii, can you share with the class your secret approach for solving problems?"

"It took me 3 full weeks to solve the problem with the sum of the row. When I am working on a difficult problem I take a paper out of my bag and don't finish until it is solved, no matter how long it takes."

In 8th grade I became the best student in my math class. By the end of school I had won numerous math competitions. I graduated from the most prestigious technical college in the country and studied in the same group with winners of international school Olympiads in math and programming.

I am insanely grateful to Alexander for showing what success is early in my life. You know why? Because success can be replicated and the process of achieving it in any area is the same.

I repeated what I learned while learning math in IT while working as an engineer at Cisco Systems. I repeated the same process when applying to one of the best MBA programs in the USA, and I repeated it in karate school and it always worked.

In my life I never relied on talent because I know that I am not particularly talented in anything. When I want something really badly I rely on the process that I came to at the age of 12: "I start working on achieving my dream and don't stop until it comes true and it doesn't matter how long it takes."

I hope that impromptu speaking skills will help you in whatever you do. No matter how long it takes, don't stop working towards your dream until it comes true. Luck smiles on the stubborn ones.

Final thoughts

Obviously, impromptu speaking overlaps with prepared public speaking in many regards. I highly recommend you read *Magic of Public Speaking: A Complete System to Become a World Class Speaker*. By using this system, you can unleash your public speaking potential in a very short period of time.

True mastery comes with practice. Join a nearby Toastmasters club and volunteer as often as possible to speak impromptu. Find like-minded friends and practice different questions and exercises together.

After some time, the techniques you learned in *Magic of Impromptu Speaking* will become part of you. To learn more recent tips and techniques I encourage you to visit my website at www.MagicOfPublicSpeaking.com.

If you enjoyed reading this book as much as I enjoyed writing it, I would appreciate your honest review on Amazon.

One Last Thing …

There is nothing more pleasant for a teacher than to see his students succeed. Begin implementing the *Magic of Impromptu Speaking* techniques in your next impromptu speech and send me an email with your success story to andrii@magicofpublicspeaking.com. I hope to hear from you soon!

Top 100 table topic questions for practice

After a certain amount of practice, you will notice some patterns in topics and genres of questions. The number of completely different questions you may be asked is limited and by practicing you may exhaust all of them.

In this section you will find 100 interesting questions and statements that you can use for practice in a group of fellow impromptu speakers. Your goal is either to answer a question or to share your opinion about a statement in the form of a short speech.

1. Who was your hero when you were a child?

2. Which historical figure do you find the most interesting?

3. Do you think we should have censorship?

4. Do you support the death sentence?

5. What is your view on gun control?

6. You should always tell the truth because ...

7. Is marriage an outdated institution?

8. Females make better bosses.

9. Do prisons serve a useful purpose in our society?

10. Money can buy anything and everything.

11. To me, success in life means ...

12. Why are people afraid to fail?

13. What does Christmas mean to you?

14. The best thing about our nation …

15. The worst problem facing our nation today …

16. Are prisons the answer for reducing crime?

17. What can we do to improve the education system?

18. The world seems to be getting smaller because …

19. Is it important to know a second language?

20. Is TV worth watching?

21. Are politics and honesty incompatible?

22. The Olympic Games – how important are they?

23. Is it OK for men to cry?

24. Should the budget for the space program be increased?

25. Should all nuclear weapons be eliminated?

26. What is your biggest regret?

27. The thing I'm most proud of.

28. What makes you happy?

29. What is your favorite travel destination?

30. What is the best movie you have ever seen?

31. What was your favorite subject at school?

32. What is the best meal you ever ate?

33. What has been your most interesting journey?

34. What was your most frightening experience?

35. Who has been the main role model in your life?

36. If I could only accomplish one thing in my life, I would like to …

37. If I were an author, I would write about …

38. If you could be an animal, what would it be?

39. If you had to be a zookeeper for a week, which animals would you prefer to look after?

40. If the world were going to end next week, what would be the last 3 things you do?

41. The best job in the world is...

42. If you didn't need to sleep, how would your life be different?

43. If you had to choose between being smarter or better-looking, which would you choose?

44. Suppose you could go back in time and talk to yourself at the age of 10. What advice would you give yourself?

45. Imagine you have just won the Mr. or Miss Universe pageant, a beauty and talent contest. You need to give a speech on television, expressing how happy you are, saying what the award means to you and thanking everyone.

46. If you were given one million dollars and had to spend it in a month, what would you do?

47. A journey of a thousand miles begins with a single step.

48. If you consult enough experts, it is possible to confirm any opinion.

49. The journey is more important than the destination.

50. A smooth path might get you there faster, but a rough trail teaches you more.

51. If a penguin entered the room, what would you say?

52. Do you think professional athletes are overpaid?

53. If you could do something dangerous just once, without any risk, what would you do?

54. If you could change one thing about the world, what would it be?

55. If you had 6 months with no obligations or financial constraints, what would you do with the time?

56. Is it more fun to be a parent or a child?

57. Who did you want to become when you were a child?

58. Who has been an inspiration to you?

59. Wealth is a means to happiness.

60. Courage is …

61. Where would you choose to live if you had to leave this country?

62. What is your most prized possession?

63. If you had to choose one word to describe yourself, which would you choose and why?

64. Describe a time when you felt really happy about yourself.

65. What excites you?

66. What is the best book you ever read?

67. What is your favorite sport?

68. My most memorable holiday is …

69. Which country would you most like to visit?

70. What do you do for fun and why?

71. I plan to retire early so that I can …

72. The world seems to be getting smaller because …

73. If you could turn back time, what age would you want to be, and why?

74. If I could be president for a day, I'd …

75. Knowledge is power.

76. When you cease to dream you cease to live.

77. Things that are easy are seldom worthwhile.

78. Why do you think Mona Lisa was smiling?

79. Where does the road less traveled lead?

80. You're 15 years old. Convince your parents to let you get a tattoo.

81. Home is where the heart is.

82. The best things in life are free.

83. You can if you think you can.

84. Time and tide wait for no man.

85. Less is more.

86. Imagine the world as a single country. Would it be good for humankind?

87. Which difficulty in life made you stronger?

88. What is the key to happiness?

89. If you were selected to go to the moon with a companion of your choice, who would you choose?

90. If you could be invisible for a day, what would you do?

91. You live next to a nuclear power plant. Defend the place as a nice place to live.

92. Success is a process, not a destination.

93. Your worth consists of what you are and not what you have.

94. The person who says that something can't be done should never interrupt the person who is doing it.

95. If you could meet any celebrity, who would it be?

96. If you could witness one event in history, which would it be?

97. If I were the opposite gender, I'd …

98. Are demonstrations a waste of time?

99. What is the best or worst present you ever received?

100. What was your favorite subject in school?

If there were a program for impromptu speaking at the university, I would give a degree in it only after you answered all 100 questions in this book. The questions are the most interesting, unusual and versatile that I could find. Once you have answered them using the techniques learned in this book, you can truly award yourself a Masters in Impromptu Speaking and this skill will stay with you forever.

What to read next?

If you enjoyed this book, you will also like *Magic of Public Speaking: A Complete System to Become a World Class Speaker*. By using this system, you can unleash your public speaking potential in a very short period of time.

Another interesting book is *Magic of Speech Evaluation: Gain World Class Public Speaking Experience by Evaluating Successful Speakers*. While reading Magic of Speech Evaluation you will watch and evaluate 15 short speeches of successful speakers. By the end of the book you will be able to clearly see what makes each speech effective and what can improve it even further. This ability will make you a more experienced speaker who can create captivating speeches on a first attempt.

Magic of Public Speaking

A Complete System to Become a World Class Speaker

The Magic of Public Speaking is a comprehensive step-by-step system for creating highly effective speeches. It is based on research from the top 1000 speakers in the modern world. The techniques you will learn have been tested on hundreds of professional speakers and work! You will receive the exact steps needed to create a speech that will keep your audience on the edge of their seats. The book is easy to follow, entertaining to read and uses many examples from real speeches. This system will make sure that every time you go on stage your speech is an outstanding one.

Magic of Speech Evaluation

Gain World Class Public Speaking Experience by Evaluating Successful Speakers

What if you could get more public speaking experience after 10 hours of reading a book than the majority of speakers get after 10 months of speaking from stage?

After reading Magic of Speech Evaluation you will have acquired the experience of applying the most effective public speaking techniques used by 1000 of the world's best speakers in various contexts. You will be able to clearly see what makes each speech effective and what can improve it even further. This ability will make you a more experienced speaker who can create a captivating speech from the first attempt.

Magic of Speech Evaluation contains numerous demonstrations of common mistakes that speakers make and effective applications of public speaking principles. After evaluating 15 short speeches of successful speakers you will develop the ability to clearly see how to improve your own speeches.

You will master 3 enormously powerful public speaking principles that are more effective than all other techniques combined. In addition, you will learn a highly effective evaluation system that will allow you to make other speakers successful.

Reading this book might not make you a world-class speaker instantly, however it will definitely get you several steps closer to this goal.

Biography

At the age of 19, Andrii obtained his CCIE (Certified Cisco Internetwork Expert) certification, the most respected certification in the IT world, and became the youngest person in Europe to hold it.

At the age of 23, he joined an MBA program at one of the top 10 MBA schools in the USA as the youngest student in the program, and at the age of 25 he joined Cisco Systems' Head Office as a Product Manager responsible for managing a router which brought in $1 billion in revenue every year.

These and other experiences have taught Andrii that success in any endeavor doesn't as much depend on the amount of experience you have but rather on the processes that you are using. Having dedicated over 10 years to researching behavior of world's most successful people and testing a variety of different techniques, Andrii has uncovered principles that will help you to unleash your potential and fulfill your dreams in a very short period of time.

Printed in Great Britain
by Amazon